CTRL

Essays on Video Games

CTRL

Essays on Video Games

Edited by Dean Fee

THE LILLIPUT PRESS
DUBLIN

First published 2026 by
THE LILLIPUT PRESS
62–63 Sitric Road,
Arbour Hill,
Dublin 7,
Ireland
www.lilliputpress.ie

10 9 8 7 6 5 4 3 2 1

A CIP record for this title is available from The British Library.

Paperback ISBN 978 1 84351 976 8
eBook ISBN 978 1 84351 992 8

Lilliput gratefully acknowledges the financial support of the Arts Council / An Chomhairle Ealaíon.
Set in 12 pt on 16 pt Adobe Caslon Pro, Zrnic and Compacta by Compuscript
This digtially-printed edition printed and bound by Lightning Source

CONTENTS

Introduction	*Dean Fee*	I
Name Your Character	*John Patrick McHugh*	9
A Branching Story	*Joe Dunthorne*	29
Don't They Know It's the End of the World? The Hell of *Fallout's Dead Money*	*Lisa McInerney*	38
Tip of My Joystick	*Sheila Armstrong*	54
A Bad Case	*Darragh McCausland*	77
A Hell Taxonomy (On Doom, 1993)	*Roisin Kiberd*	90
Chasing Lilacs	*Brenda Romero*	III
To Wander, To Stop	*Chandrika Narayanan-Mohan*	125
Mega Dreoilín	*Donal Fullam*	137

CONTENTS

Tomb Raider, Remastered   *Anna Loughran*   149

So Long Nerds   *Paul Whyte*   162

Your Job Sucks?
Try Working in Games   *Úna-Minh Kavanagh*   178

Childish Things: My Life
in Computer Games   *Rob Doyle*   190

World Warriors   *Stephen Sexton*   207

INTRODUCTION

Dean Fee

When I made my Confirmation in 1999, the only thing I wanted was to make enough money to buy a Game Boy Colour and *Pokémon Red Version*. I didn't care about being initiated into the Catholic Church. I didn't care about becoming a man in the eyes of God. I didn't care about making the Pledge to not drink or do drugs until I was eighteen. All I wanted was to be the greatest Pokémon trainer there ever was. In cream trousers and a granddad shirt, I stayed close to my mother while we kept an eye out for my father coming over from Dundalk. He hadn't arrived by the time my class was ushered in the door, but Mam assured me he'd be there in time. In the church, at the end of the pews there were cards taped with the names of my classmates as well as some kids from sur-rounding schools. Before I found my own name, my mother found hers. She was delighted at first – happy to be known – and then confused as I explained that there was a girl in my class who shared her name. I'd probably told her this ten times.

I sat down and waited, and when the time came I joined my classmates in the aisle and we all stepped slowly towards the priest, who was mumbling prayers and handing out holy bread. When it was my turn I looked as pious as I could and offered my cupped hands as a receptacle for the body of Christ. Kneeling then in the pew, pretending to pray, I worked the shape of it from the roof of my mouth with my tongue and swallowed. The priest ended the ceremony and we all flooded out into the carpark. My dad was there and he asked if I'd taken my pledge. I said I had, and when I swore I'd stick to it, he laughed and, with confidence, said he'd give me fifty quid if I did. I obviously lost that bet.

The Game Boy Colour plus the Pokémon game were priced at €110. The closest place that sold them was the Argos, over an hour away, in Blanchardstown shopping centre. My mother had promised to drive me there the following day, provided I made the money. All around me my friends were making money hand over fist. In the hallways of the town's hotel they told me numbers. They said things like one fifty and two hundred; they said they had a cousin who, last year, made almost five big ones. No one believed this, but at the end of the day, when I saw I'd only made eighty, I believed well enough that there was someone out there with five hundred.

Time ticked on and, in a last bid to achieve my goal, I pulled on my father's sleeve and told him my plight. He didn't understand what these things I wanted were. He thought I had made enough money and told me that on his Confirmation day he made one pound and was sent straight back home to work on the farm.

I was crushed.

I was defeated.

I thought it was game over until, just as I turned away to go sulk in some corner, my father said, Hold on, and from the back pocket of his jeans he pulled his black wallet and asked again how much I needed. I said a number and he handed me the notes, withholding them for a moment to remind me that I couldn't say he never did anything for me. He would do similar in the twenty-plus years to come—when I needed money for college, for the bus, for rent, for food—but this is the one I remember. I gave him a hug and he told me to go on.

The next day's drive to Blanchardstown was a slow agony. In Argos I flipped the heavy catalogue to the page I knew so well and copied the reference number onto the docket. I expected the woman at the counter to understand the significance of the moment, but instead she took my money, gave me a number, and told me to go and sit and wait. When my number was called I collected the package from the counter and ran to meet my mother. She must have been in a hurry because before I knew it I was bundled into the car. We were already on the motorway by the time I tore open the box and saw they have given me the wrong thing. Instead of the new, in-colour Game Boy, they gave me the older, black-and-white screened

Game Boy Pocket. They gave me the wrong thing, I said, but it was too late. We couldn't turn around now.

As tragic as that sounds, it didn't turn out too badly. There were benefits to having a black and white screen. For one, it came with a contrast wheel that, when playing the slot machines in Celadon City, could be darkened in such a way that it was easier to land the 777 that would eventually lead me to getting enough money to buy a Porygon; or could be lightened and angled this way and that to allow me to continue to play in the near-dark.

Pokémon was the first game I became addicted to. I played it day and night and, reading through the work in this anthology I'm relieved to see how universal my experience was. Much like John Patrick McHugh with his beloved *Final Fantasy IX*, when *Pokémon* was taken from me, I continued to hear the game's music in my head. I was convinced the game had been left on and was hidden somewhere. I searched high and low and at one point found myself with my head stuck under my aunty's kitchen sink, my ears cocked for the phantom melody, the wee hours of the morning fading towards daylight.

Since I wasn't allowed to play the game, I satiated myself by writing about it. With a pen and a hardback notebook I climbed into the cubby hole under our stairs, where my family stored all the rubbish we couldn't bear to throw away, and rewrote the game's story. I was essentially writing fan fiction, but at the time all I wanted was to be inside that world again. Except this time, without the constraints of the game's strict linear narrative, I could do whatever I wanted. Instead of one of the classic starter Pokémon (Squirtle, Bulbasaur, Charmander), I chose a Sandshrew to be my first companion. Instead of leaving from Pallet Town and kissing my Mom goodbye, my character was from Vermilion City and my father worked on the *S.S. Anne*. Instead of being gifted a bike from the head of the Pokémon Fan Club, I stole one.

Ever since then I've loved narrative-driven games, whether they be linear stories like *Final Fantasy* or *Red Dead Redemption*, or open-ended games like *World of Warcraft* or *Football Manager* where with every move I make I chose my own narrative. To my mind writing and gaming go hand-in-hand. Both are interested in progression, both are interested in story and both are done with artistic intent, for the most part.

Over a few drinks one afternoon in Letterkenny, Co. Donegal, Stephen Sexton (who has written an excellent piece for this anthology) told me about a game he'd played in his youth and had been trying to find again. Much like the people in Sheila Armstrong's piece about the Reddit page r/tipofmyjoystick, he only knew a few details, snatches of memory that didn't quite fill out the shape of the game he remembered. After a long time searching he found something, something that he could not deny was the game he had been looking for, only it didn't quite live up to his memory of it. Hoping for instant recollection and – I'll presume – a transportation back to his childhood, he was left disappointed, regretting ever seeking it out. If he had left it alone his memory would have persisted, there to revisit as he pleased.

Like any other art form, the games we play are always encountered within the context of our own lives. The pieces written for this anthology explore this in a way I could never have expected. In Paul Whyte's essay 'So Long Nerds' he recounts playing *Metal Gear Solid: Peace Walker* 'sitting in a sterile room inside St Vincent's Hospital, waiting for my father-in-law to finish his chemotherapy'. Daragh McCausland plays *Disco Elysium* in his childhood bedroom whilst trying to overcome alcohol addiction. After a period of intense burnout, Chandrika Narayanan-Mohan plays *Wanderstop*, a game about that very experience. In a squat in Dublin, Donal Fullam creates a game that skewers the very housing crisis he's living through. In Rob Doyle's piece he recounts almost his entire life through the games he has played. I sat in my cubby hole with my knees up and played my Game Boy while around me the century turned. I travelled back and forth between Cavan and Louth, in and out of the custody of my parents. Gaming for me and for a lot of people was about escape, but more than that it was about control. Whether it was the tiny portable screen or the vast flatscreen TV, there was always a world waiting where I was in charge, a place where I knew every nook and cranny, where, much like how we rewatch favourite movies or TV shows, I could go for a sense of comfort. In Anna Loughran's piece about the remastered *Tomb Raider* series, she explores how we rewrite the narratives of our youth and asks how much we can trust our memories. Is it even possible to relive them?

Video games are often an extension of our tastes. In Lisa McInerney's essay about the *Fallout: New Vegas* DLC *Dead Money*, her interest in the end of the world, sparked by books like *Z for Zachariah* and *Children of the Dust*, is expanded. Here she gets to, in some small way, live it. And with taste comes the urge to create, and what writer/gamer hasn't wanted to try their hand at making a game themselves. In 'A Branching Narrative' Joe Dunthorne writes about an attempt to create an 'an interactive, permutable story' that almost drove him mad. Both Úna-Minh Kavanagh and Donal Fullam give us a glimpse behind the curtain and show us the great effort required to bring these games to light. And in the wonderful alchemy of it all, games designer Brenda Romero presents her own personal history through a video game structure.

My initial idea for this anthology was simple: to gather a collection of writing that used video games as a cipher, as a way to trace the personal histories of our lives. In doing so, I felt certain that this book would make some small case for video games to be seen as an artistic medium. Rather than straight-up asking that burning question however, these essays look at video games as fascinating aspects our lives more broadly. They look at how they weave in and out of our conversations, our anecdotes, our memories. Though they are places where we can play – with our friends, fighting or working together; alone living out fantasies; or simply problem-solving – these writers also recognise their capacity to be destructive and addictive. They *can* bring joy, and as Roisin Kiberd says in her essay, have 'transformative potential', but they can also offer easy comfort and a seductively easy place to dwell too long.

I have personally dwelt too long in some worlds, sacrificing time with my family, cancelling plans with friends, closing the curtains and surrendering entire days to the pull of an easier life, one where I worry not so much about the real world. We use and depend on video games in many ways. Some of us use them to socialize, some of us depend on them to get away from it all. I think a lot of us depend on them the way we depend on any work of art, to remind us of the human capacity for creativity and joy. Either way you look at it, games have become a vital part of our lives, a force to be reckoned with and one that's not going away any time soon. Whether it's triple A blockbusters you like, or small indie games with heart, within these pages I feel confident you'll find a reflection of your own life, evidence of some connecting tissue that binds us. That's why we tell stories. That's why we play.

NAME YOUR CHARACTER

John Patrick McHugh

Dragon

Hear a raging storm, hear gale and thunderous wave, and then see it. Grey sea and spray and pelting rain, and there, amongst it, rocking and swirling, a small rickety boat with a single sail. Now watch a wave build and build and toss the boat as if it were a toy. A flash of thunder. See a hooded woman and child struggling to pilot the thrown boat. Another flash: note the anguish writ on the woman's face. Black and cut to a waking princess: a silver crown of knots and jewels, a strapless ballgown. Rose gold light streams into her bedroom and now hear music for the first time, hear doves chirping, as the princess rises and pushes open a window. See a castle, its great walls and gates and four turrets, and further on the moat and canals, the packed-in townhouses with brick-red roofs and shuttered windows, the windmill and gushing waterfalls, the mist bubbling up from the gorge below, and see too the gigantic sword protruding heavenward from the centre of the castle. The music is building now, but the full orchestra is yet to play. The strings swoon and instantly drop, and then trumpets and drums suddenly sound. Now see another ship: an impressive galleon. A stone mermaid is perched on its prow, and the doves are sailing alongside it. See spinning propellers, see the wheels and levers in the bright windows above the deck. Watch the galleon fly astoundingly through cloud and sky and towards the castle as the music swells. And now *be* the boy with the monkey tail, sliding down the firepole inside the galleon. Listen to the groan of the airborne ship as you control him in a gloomy screen. Move and discover the stash of Gil stowed in the far corner, then pick the potion hidden on the opposite side. Now heed the ghostly prompt and light the candles in the middle of the room. Appreciate the slowly revealed background: the railing hooked with outfits, the dim portrait on the wall, the boxes and knick-knacks stuffed on shelves and atop wardrobes, the rug beneath the boy's ankle boots with the heart and the ornate lettering spelling out TANTALUS. Now be ready to rename the character correctly, be prepared to battle the dragon-man: the first boss.

Attack

Final Fantasy IX is the best RPG, the best video game ever. Its story is frantic and fun – it unfolds with a whimsical scheme to kidnap royalty and climaxes with you, the player, battling Death to save the world from annihilation – and yet it often slackens this headlong pace to linger on tinier character moments, quieter scenes of introspection. The world of Gaia, the world you are given to explore, is crammed with secrets and moody dungeons and treasure chests to kick open. The locations you visit on your adventure are wondrous and wondrously strange: a sprawling clock-like city, an upside-down castle, a religious sect atop a tree. The inhabitants are sometimes anthropomorphic, sometimes rotund Disneyesque figures, and always charming. The music is sublime: eerie at stages, and at other stages purring to your ears like a half-remembered lullaby. The eight main characters become your friends: they are defined by their fears while simultaneously appearing like cartoons. The monster design is kooky; the big bad dungeon bosses are threatening with just the right among of quirks. The progression of your party's fighting skills is immensely satisfying: from Fire charging to Fira, then to Firaga, a Do-Re-Mi of magical spells. The baddie possesses menacing gravitas at the beginning, is sympathetic by the close. Each new screen you advance upon is baroquely detailed due to the pre-rendered backgrounds: from the lifeless blues of Terra's walkways and its towering tree-like saucers to the architect's study in the ravaged city of Burmecia with its candle flickering by the drawing board. Throughout *FFIX*, the stakes are kept excitingly high – you carry the fate of Gaia; you must confront murky questions of existence and purpose – and comically, splendidly low: will you please assist Quina in eating ninety-nine frogs so that they are bequeathed the legendary Gastro Fork?

Steal

A fat boy of nine creeps inside a garden shed. Watch as he checks over his shoulder once, twice, before crouching beside a heap of brooms and shovels and rakes in the corner. He rummages. He tests the weight of a broom and discards it, then pulls out a shovel, a twist of wrist, discards that too, and now he reaches for a sweeping brush. The boy stands, taking the handle with both hands, and swings it. Swings it again, faster. A floating wad of cobweb. Oxblood bristles. The fat boy needs to make sure that this stick isn't cumbersome, that it is not splintery to grasp. Satisfied with his choice, the boy unhooks a saw from a nail on the wall and, like a doomsday beaver, scurries out of the shed, the saw and brush under one crooked arm. He hurries to the narrow strip of garden which – he has checked, he has confirmed – lays concealed from any nosy eyes in the kitchen window. His face is blushing. He drops the broom and checks over his shoulder, once, twice. Now he grips the saw.

Skill

In theory, an RPG is a more thoughtful experience than your average video game. It is a genre built on wits and cunning and the comprehension of statistics. You can customize your characters to function how you prefer them to function. You are encouraged to plan and defuse rather than button-bash. It is essential not to outgun your adversary, but to outthink them.

In *FFIX*, this cerebral mediation occurs from the principle of turn-based combat and random encounters.

Frequently, as you are scampering through whatever destination – be it across the distinct grain of the 3D overworld or the glossy sheen of a pre-rendered background – you will hear a sudden suck of air, witness a whirlpool slurping down your screen, and you'll be whisked to a stage and a battle against a skeleton, or a glum owl, or a small furious ram, or a zombie whale, or a multiple-tentacled demon called a Malboro...

A turn-based battle is a deferential dance, an adorably unrealistic representation of hand-to-hand combat. A typical fight: the chuck-a-chuck-a of guitar and the camera spinning to a closeup of your enemy – let's say it's the boar, Zaghnol – before a panning shot of the four characters you're using. A list of names appear at the bottom of the screen, animated bars start to chug from one end to the other. As soon as the time bar fills, a pyramid popping over the readied character, you guide a gloved hand along the four-stacked menu of command and select your wisest move: if controlling Vivi you'll perhaps pick a spell, if John you might steal ore from the furry pockets of this tusked enemy. You made your choice, you press X, and you watch for the stilted animation to begin – watch Steiner hopping forward to slash at Zaghnol, or Eiko using her flute to summon a Phoenix to scorch this piggie. A number flashes – white means pain, lime-green means replenishment – and you repeat this process until the foe is vanquished: you wait for your bar to fill, you get hit, you attack or cure or use an item, and hopefully the trumpets of victory blare and your band will pose heroically for the swooping camera at the end.

In practice, during my first playthrough, I understood none of an RPG's distinctive complexities. Zero skill was involved, zero reckoning with strategy or the nuances of spells beyond the rush of their cinematics. I didn't match armours to garner add-ons that could nullify debilitating curses. I didn't consider how the buff of a lowly dagger could be more useful than the blade higher in attack power. Instead, I kept the core party – because I liked those four characters the best – and selected whatever helmet or robe sent my character's stats shooting up. I pressed attack and watched my character bonk the heads of baddies. I presumed that blunt force would win out, and when it didn't, when I was put on my arse by Kuja, or devastated by the security system in the Desert Palace, I would grind until my level was so high, my hit points so superior, that I could, once more, barrel tactlessly forward.

Summon

I wasn't bullied for being fat. I felt the pressure of it, yes, felt a searing and judgemental gaze, imagined or otherwise, upon my repulsive body, but I was not routinely called a fatty or jeered at for owning a pair of tits, or shoved about the yard. I was lucky: I was a decent-sized obstruction in goals and had high-ranking friends. There was only one moment of abuse that stands out. I was in third class and my gang were annoying a sixth-class boy nicknamed Peacock. It had been occurring irregularly over a couple of weeks – giddy, egged on by our older brothers, we would pester this unfortunate boy at big break by shouting insults – but then it escalated. I can't recall what our taunting entailed – no doubt it was horrible, probably borne from prejudice about Peacock's social class or, ironically, how he looked – but, of course, I remember when Peacock ultimately snapped back one afternoon. He swung for the loudest of us and connected and sent him tumbling, kicked out at another, and then he said to me: Fuck off, Fatty. Simple, brutal. I went cold and backed away to our share of the yard, head lowered, lip wobbling. For the rest of lunch, my group didn't mention our comeuppance. The fella who was punched pretended he had not been punched. However, once home, I squealed to my older sister. I must have exaggerated and lied, I must have guessed she knew who Peacock was from town, and that weekend she ate the poor lad. She informed Peacock to stay well clear of her brother. I was playing *Final Fantasy* – honestly – when she arrived home and told me I won't be bothered by him anymore.

Item

FFIX was released in 2000 for the PlayStation. It was SquareSoft's final hurrah to that specifically grey console before crossing over to the future and PlayStation 2. The game came in a blocky double-decker case (the heavy click to open each case and inside two shiny white discs atop one another; four in total). The cover image was plain and regal: holy-white apart from the runic-like lettering of the title with a mysterious crystal jammed in the middle.

Trance

I was addicted to the game in the weeks and months after purchase. I was suckered in by the scope, the characters, and I played till my eyeballs crisped. How hours fell in this trance. How ridiculous was my temper when I was instructed to switch it off. In bed, my head fried, I'd hear in rotating echoes the music of locales and characters from the game – the ragtime piano of Treno, the plucked strings of Steiner's theme alongside his clanking chain-mail. Soon I begged for the official guide, and would study it daily once received, delighted in reliving the game through text. I started to envision the video game world seeping over my drab real one: the thorns over the back wall of my school were actually part of the Evil Forest: I surmised that one of my detested friends would be a rat from Burmecia, and wasn't the girl I talked to not the spit of Princess Garnet? I would finish the game and take a few days off before once more climbing inside its tale of thieves and genocidal eidolons, into its gameplay loop of battling and levelling.

White Magic

The family had moved four times before we settled in Macroom, County Cork. I was eight and would receive *FFIX* about a year later. By then, I had changed school twice, had come to see friendship as a fleeting experience. I was a shy boy. In public, when not with family, I started to despise myself in abstract ways – it started with my weight but then it plunged deeper. The opening musical theme of *FFIX* – the pump-organ hum that you hear at the start menu – is entitled 'A Place to Call Home'. The overarching motif of the game is the quest for a home – figurative and literal – and the purpose such a place can provide: John is searching for his forgotten birthplace, signified by a blue light; Eiko is apparently the sole survivor of her tribe and wishes to belong somewhere else. Even if these concerns skipped over my mind when I was an obtuse young buck, it must have affected me subconsciously like a sugary-sweet Calpol to quench a pain in your ear. It would have clicked.

Help

RPG stands for role-playing game. An offspring of dice-rolling adventures, it is a genre with particular emphasis on world building and character development and story. A novelistic video game, if you will.

OK, so, in terms of geography, Gaia marries picturesque fantasy in its greenery and cutesy settlements with some gibberish sci-fi features: two moons, a tree funnelling the souls of another planet called Terra to replace the souls of Gaia. It is a medieval society: farmers and small shopkeepers and wealthy nobles. Health is administered through flasks of potions. Creatures of incomparable power – the eidolons – were summoned once upon a time by a tribe with horns poking from their foreheads. A crystal at the centre of the planet is the source of all living things. There are large rideable birds named Chocobos, helpful cats called Moogles and a family of hippos who run a popular hotel.

Now bear with me: *FFIX* follows the cheeky but endearing John (he has a monkey's tail, wears a sleeveless top with a dandy jabot, and his name might not be John in your own playthrough) as he arrives into Alexandria on a theatre ship to perform a play – but really, John alights to kidnap Princess Garnet (she is capable of summoning eidolons, as she used to have a horn). Garnet, as it transpires, wants to be abducted so that she can find a way to stop her mother, the Queen – who isn't Garnet's real mother – from inciting war between the kingdoms ruling the continent. Garnet and John are pursued by the bumbling knight Steiner (no tail or horn) and, through his own clumsiness, a magician named Vivi (picture a pointy hat and underneath a black void with yellow eyes). As the plot becomes increasingly convoluted, and as war indeed breaks out between the kingdoms, further characters join this foursome: the gluttonous Quina (clownlike with a floppy tongue), the imperturbable warrior Freya (rat with a spear), a six-year-old named Eiko (she can also summon eidolons, still has her horn) and the bounty hunter Amarant (human with teal skin). The main villain in all this is Kuja (he has a secret tail and is sort of the brother of John), whose motive advances from warmongering alongside the Queen so as to quicken the replacing of Gaia's souls with that of his home planet Terra – oh yeah, which is John's home planet, too – to simply wishing to obliterate all life once he learns his mortality is prearranged and approaching.

Are you still with me?

Black Magic

In writing about this video game, I am writing about me as a boy playing this video game, and in replaying *FFIX* today – which I am doing on the pretext of research – I am experiencing it as that boy once more. A video game as hardened memory. My adoration of *FFIX* ascends beyond the game's strengths. It is about the safety and security that swells up when I periodically wonder if I should dip back into Gaia. In other words, it is now nostalgia. It is the exact rot that I associate with the legion of superhero flicks – a cultural item that is unsurprising and intellectually boring. I play *FFIX* because I don't want to be challenged. I play *FFIX* because I want everything to be under my direct control. I play *FFIX* because I want to be a child – carefree, innocent, etc. It is a reactionary impulse. I should stop but I will not; I will continue to play it, year after year.

Focus

It was in fourth class in my all-boys school, when we turned ten and started to smell a little sour, that I became fat. Before then I was tubby, was breasted, was double chinned. But it wasn't until girls transitioned from slight novelty into the essential variable within our equations for what we should do against what was considered lame and shitty that I felt fat to the world. My weight was now public, intentional. I was an embarrassment not only to myself but to my friends. I was a stink as we glared up at the girls' school on our hike to the library. I was the reason why girls were unattainable to us. And on those rare times when we encountered girls, I could sense trouble, I could interpret my new troubling position: now I swayed between friend and useful target. If these girls were to speak to us, I was a ready-made punchline for my boys to fill space with. I was sure about this tacit betrayal because I was searching for a lad beneath me to use. I was just as traitorous.

Sword Art

In that unspyable slice of garden around the side of the house, I chopped the head off the stolen brush. Tossing the bristled end, I picked up the handle and slashed it left and right. The air whistled. I thumped the stick against the coal bunker, smiling at the drum of impact. Held it at one end and let the stick slide through my palms until I grasped it at its very centre. I twirled it then like a baton before bringing it to rest aside my hip as I pivoted into a samurai stance – left arm forward and fingers gesturing cooly for my enemy to come get some.

While I played like this, I was constantly checking for watchers in the windows, in the surrounding estate. I would throw the stick aside if I heard approaching footfall, or the back door, or tyres flinging gravel along our road. I would keep a football close by – an inconspicuous out. At some point, my Nana came to stay with us, and I recall coming to despise her – my beloved Nana! – because she enjoyed sitting by the sunlit window in the spare room. In this, she threatened to reveal my bizarre world.

She would wave as I stamped about damning her soul, the stick stiff in my hand.

Obviously, I was nowhere near as discreet as I presumed. My father has a video of me thrashing my stick at no one. You can hear him whisper before he unlatches the window: 'we'll see now if he has his stick with him'. A space was arranged in the shed where I could deposit my deadly arsenal; my parents would shout to check that I was alive in my patch of garden; my sister lumped me over the head with one of my secret sticks during an argument.

Sword Magic

So what was I at with the headless brushes and brooms? It was quite innocent. It is mortifying. Simply: the numerous sticks I collected became a knight's broadsword, a dragoon's javelin, a thief's dagger in my private theatre. It wasn't so much imagination: rather they were those weapons to me then. How do I explain that? Prove it? I can't. Once I picked up those sticks they were pronged and weighty and I was whatever hero in whatever current act of my drama. For those hours spent swinging my weapons, I would mutter the voices and narration for tales inspired by *FFIX* – I'd employ the same peaks and troughs of its plot, use its varied landscape – but with sprinklings of originality: I'd make up a new evil baddie, new backstories for those characters I thought were underdeveloped, new dungeons. No audience, but I was immersed in these performances. Like when playing the video game: I wasn't me.

All these stories concluded in much the same fashion: the hero discovers love in the princess from Alexandria. After he defeats the climactic boss, he pledges devotion to her for now and forever – the Ultima Weapon still in his hands – and this princess declares her own love for him. These romantic moments never rushed beyond the promise of an unbreakable bond, a cuddle. It was simple confirmation that one person loved the other person, and my story would end right there – to be started all over again the next day.

Jump

The triumph of hearing the ping that confirms you have levelled up. The excitement of seeing your HP jumping from 930 to 971 as the corner rolls from level 19 to 20. Can I explain this rapture properly, when all it really means is that I'm a little bit harder to kill, a little bit more powerful? How do I convey the buzz in studying the slightest increase in stats like Attack and Defence, Magic and Spirit? I suppose it is like scoring a goal: no words can do justice to the elation. So you must go do it: you must grind, have your character run in circles and fight the same crop of enemies again and again and again and again and again. Only then will you soar as I soar when the experience points drop and the level springs up.

Eat

The two emotions I associate with being fat are fear and shame.

The fear sprung from the knowledge that if I spoke out of line in a group, I could be, I would be, slapped back down into my lowly place. Without much thought on their part, without much malice, I could be made to feel ugly, pathetic, worthless – which is what I felt about myself. Everyone could do me. I could perform the greatest feat imaginable – saving a peno, throwing a rubber at the back of someone's head in the middle of class – and still, with one half-baked insult, I would be done.

The shame arose in trivial matters. In the dressing room, for example, I would panic over which jerseys were bundled inside the duffel bag: the newish ones, which were comfortable and baggy? Or the woollen jerseys, which were long-armed yet skin-tight, which made me look like a freak? And as a result of the trivial becoming degrading, shame came to slowly warp all public bouts of spontaneous joy – I could never fully experience happiness while surrounded by others, because it could scald as soon as it cheered.

Take Speech and Drama in school, a class I adored: the chance to act the maggot and be clapped at. Each year, there was a competition held in Cork, and on the day when we were due to sing and dance to 'Circle of Life', I was informed I would be wearing an off-the-shoulder Lycra top with leopard print. (I still question what they were thinking in pushing such clothing: was it a sort of joke for the overseeing adults, the fat kid in Lycra?) The top clung to my body, highlighted the rolls along my stomach, built sacks out of my chest. In the bathroom, I cried while staring at the mirror, and once backstage in the theatre in Cork, I hid in a corner and hoped I'd be forgotten, that my space would be automatically filled by someone else. When the bell sounded, and the teacher angrily told me to get ready pronto, I asked could I please not wear this top. For the first time in my life, I admitted aloud to the humiliation of my body – how excruciating it was to have this type of body. Before classmates dressed as animals and Tarzans, I pleaded, and I was told to cop on. This woman said: Will you hurry up and change.

Blue Magic

In my bedroom, I would practise John's poses from cutscenes and in-game set pieces. I'd mimic his leave-it-to-me chest thump, his ready-for-a-brawl squat. I'd even attempt to run like him: the OTT lope like a rocking horse. I had changed the name within the game to my own, and now I sought to adjust the real-life John to be more like *FFIX*'s superior version.

Flair

While I was pitching this essay, my editor (Danny Denton, *The Stinging Fly*) remarked on a *Final Fantasy* title he himself had loved: *Final Fantasy VII*. *VII* is the loftier brother of *IX*. It is a darker RPG: the 'princess' in *VII* is impaled by a katana. The editor mentioned that his experience with *FFVII* had been more affecting than with any book he had encountered as a teenager. I hadn't considered this notion or thought it could be a notion to consider – that a game could have a valuable impact on imagination and creativity – but it was strikingly true for me as well. I can remember only one book I read during the blurry run of five to eleven years old, but I recall every character beat that happened in *FFIX*, every little scene. The style I look for in books today, the very stuff I seek to replicate in my own work, can be traced back to *FFIX* and what it introduced me to: slightly off-humour, tiny character moments, perplexed protagonists, the concurrent High and Low.

More broadly, when I peel beyond narrative preferences, when I look truthfully at myself, as a person, the game has had an undue impact on how I consider life. It is shameful to admit this, but a lot of my deliberate 'philosophical' outlook is derived from the John in *FFIX*, and his moral tagline: You don't need a reason to help people. It is a simple credo, naïve – Barney the Dinosaur probably pronounced similar in a song – but it is an attitude I cling to.

Change

We said good luck to Cork when I was twelve, moving to Galway to live with my grandparents. Over my last summer in Cork, without any dietary change, I lost a power of weight. It was never remarked upon at home; it didn't feel like an accomplishment on my behalf, it just happened. So when I arrived in Galway, I was no longer podgy, chubby, fat. While not skinny, I was not notably titted in my new school jumper, not figured for a goalie in the yard. As I went about in public, it didn't seem as if strangers wanted to destroy me. I made new friends. I joined a football club as an outfield player.

My obsession with video games ebbed away around this point, too. I still bought a couple, but I stopped getting the magazines. Games were not considered cool in primary school, nor in my secondary school, and to fit in, I suppressed all gaming knowledge beyond the latest *FIFA* and *GTA* – in the same way I would pretend to enjoy techno music for a stretch in my teens. I did try out the new *Final Fantasy* games and enjoyed *X* – John now had blonde-tipped hair – but never got on with the rest: the freedom and self-expression I had found in *IX* wasn't present in the newer ones, mainly because voice-acting was dominant, character's names were set in stone, and so your own imagination was less useful.

Throw

Occasionally, throughout my teens, I would throw up after a meal. Now and then, I would feel certain I was becoming fat, fatter, and I'd find myself kneeling by a toilet with my head tipped forward and two fingers in my throat. I would gag and retch and vomit bile and chunks of food. The sudden slosh of this acidic mixture, the gasp for air between rounds. I'd repeat this action five to six times and once content with the amount of food discharged, I would wipe the slime from my mouth and the rim of the toilet, unstick wayward nuggets of food from the bowl. Then I'd flush, and flush once more for luck.

This expulsion wasn't done regularly enough for me to think of it as a problem. I would just do it, as I said, now and then, because I didn't want to be fat, get fatter, I didn't want to experience being that John again.

Defend

Oh, *FFIX* is undeniably a slow game. And yes, the persistent random encounters become a pain. The battles themselves are often formulaic affairs – hit the attack button, wait for your turn, hit attack once more. The plot relies on the villain explaining his scheme to the camera while atop a dragon. The limitations of the hardware – how much the PlayStation could handle on screen, how many unique models it could process – are a further hurdle to traverse. Yes, the Chocobo Hot and Cold is an arduous side quest. Fair enough, the dungeons are quite straightforward: the puzzles never exceptionally taxing. And on closer examination, *FFIX* is nowhere near as wonderfully expansive as you presume it to be – in fact, it is quite linear: the story shuttles you briskly along from point A to point B to a boss battle; repeat.

Escape

… is the purpose of *Final Fantasy*, the purpose of video games. To escape and explore a more interesting world. To escape and accomplish things I could not accomplish in real life. To escape and not be myself – or, better, to be somebody else.

In the years since my first lumbering playthrough, I have replayed *FFIX* an insane number of times. I have beaten it on the PlayStation 2 and 3, the lappie, an iPhone after a day spent selling schoolbooks. I have perused the

Final Fantasy wiki into the wee small hours. I have read nonsensical theories that seek to fill *FFIX* plot holes, to enhance the lore. I listen to the game's soundtrack when writing, while writing this essay. When I feel uncommonly sad, I search for my favourite cutscenes on YouTube – and while watching all thirty-nine minutes of the ending sequence, I still swoon like a lonely child when the princess leaps into John's arms. I know the game off by heart – though when I suffer a memory lapse, I will pause and consult my guide. There is no challenge, I want no challenge. It is an automated experience. And yet, despite the many years, as soon as the theme music chimes, I'm no longer me. Instead, I am that better John, whose personality is charming and brash, whose actions are virtuous, who is skinny and likeable. There is glory when I step through the Ice Cavern and the entire world of Gaia opens up and out for me and my party of adventurers: the domed huts of the bucolic village of Dali in the distance, the lump of rock that is Observatory Mountain, the foggy valley far below and its deep, dark woods, the field of stippled green and olive that I must now traverse, the nooks and hollows that I must explore, the mightiest monsters that I must slay.

A BRANCHING STORY

Joe Dunthorne

On Christmas Day in 1992, my parents gave me a computer game. The game was called *Turrican II: The Final Fight*, and I knew from reading recent copies of *Zzap!64* magazine that it was regarded as the crowning achievement of Manfred Trenz, the greatest programmer of his generation. Saying Trenz's name out loud in the playground could cause sun-deprived children to stop still and give thanks that they lived in the era of true artistic greatness. The game's cover showed a biomechanical man-machine roaring in existential pain. After spending the minimum polite amount of time in my parents' company, I disappeared upstairs to play it in my attic room and remained there, cross-legged in front of the screen, into the evening and all through the night without pause or hydration, only returning downstairs just before lunch on Boxing Day as the smell of microwaved leftovers rose through the house. Stewed cabbage, my madeleine. When I entered the kitchen, my parents – who had not been concerned by my absence – simply asked me to set the table. Couldn't they tell that I had travelled to the year 3025 and died a hundred times? I understood in that moment that there was an uncrossable distance between us.

When I was interviewed twenty-six years later for a job writing the script of a new video game, I mentioned a version of this anecdote. I was trying to flag up my inherent nerdiness, but what I didn't realize was that games had moved on. Or at least they were trying to. My interviewers explained that their project wasn't aimed at hardcore or even casual gamers but, rather, at people like my parents. The game's characters weren't space marines or mutants but a family living in contemporary Wales and, in fact, I was advised not to call it a game at all – it was an 'interactive drama'. They made it clear that the last thing the project needed was another gamer. They wanted me for my mundane domestic fiction. I asked them how much of the existing story I would be allowed to change and they said everything. They asked me if I wanted to read the abandoned script of the previous writer – the writer they'd just fired, the body beneath the floorboards – and I said no thanks.

In a spare meeting room we called 'the cave' – to make a feature of it having no windows – I started from scratch. In planning an interactive, permutable story, the important thing was to find interesting dilemmas for the player to decide on the protagonist's behalf. Many of the choices I created were to do with how the protagonist should communicate with his family. What secrets should he hide? What should he share? What version of ourselves do we allow others to see? How much of our loved ones' hidden selves do we really want to uncover? And if this description seems a bit vague to you then you've picked up on the fact that, when I got the job, I was required to sign an intimidating ten-page non-disclosure agreement. As such, I cannot use, modify, copy, reduce to writing, record, distribute, sublicense or create derivative works from anything I wrote, read or saw during my time in the unnamed location working on the unnamed project with the unnamed colleagues. (Perhaps this explains why the game's central narrative became increasingly about secrecy: hiding my work life from friends and family at least counted as research.)

Even though most of the individual choices I outlined were simple and binary – should you lie or confess? fight or flee? – they quickly accumulated into a complex network. At the end of the first draft, there were more than a hundred thousand potential story pathways. The walls of the room were postered with forking branches of possible outcomes, colour-coded Post-its, lengths of string stretched between drawing pins like a homicide detective's cork board. My colleagues had to stick a note on the door telling the cleaners not to instinctively dump it all in the bin.

One of the big challenges when writing a branching narrative is that, ideally, every outcome should be equally satisfying. In reality, of course, this is impossible. There were branches I loved and those I found embarrassing. If

I were working on a novel, I'd obviously cut the weaker branches but, in this case, I not only had to keep them, I had to spend the majority of my time trying to salvage them, expending huge effort on storylines I dearly hoped no human would ever see. And whenever I tried to subtly direct players towards what I deemed the 'best' story, my colleagues reminded me about one of the central difficulties of video game design. While many players will earnestly engage with the game (making decisions for a character based on how they would behave in a similar situation) and others, like myself, will be led purely by a sense of entertainment (the pleasure, for example, of watching a character make terrible life decisions), there is also a notable minority whose guiding principles are perversity and chaos. They get their kicks from mocking the game designers' intentions. On YouTube you can watch videos of these kinds of players squealing as they throw grenades at the hostages they are supposed to be saving, measuring their success by their comrades' howls of outrage. Whatever the game designer wants for them is what they most hope to destroy.

Accordingly, I learned to treat players as one might parent a teenager. Let them make their own mistakes. Respect them, even when their behaviour is preposterous and childish. Don't push too hard or they'll rebel. And at the end of it all, understand that whatever they choose – if they torch the school just because it will look pretty as it burns – then their life, their choices, remain your responsibility. It was possible, for instance, for players to get the protagonist killed halfway through the narrative.

If they really, really tried, he could end up bleeding out at an airport transfer bus stop, ending the story prematurely and ruining all my beautiful character arcs and nuanced final-act reveals. Though it was tempting to deny the player the option of butchering the story in this way, I was made to understand that it was necessary because – in order for the protagonist's survival to feel earned – it also had to be possible for him to die. There can be no wisdom without stupidity.

As I was writing the protagonist's bus stop death monologue, the whole floor of my office began to be refurbished – everything except for 'the cave'. Day by day, my colleagues decamped upstairs, and the desks, sofas and computers steadily disappeared until I was left alone in a large, empty open-plan workspace the size of two tennis courts, light flooding through floor-to-ceiling windows framing a beautiful view which each morning I ignored, entering instead the small, windowless meeting room to work on the part of the story I most disliked. Though it's normal to go a little insane while writing any large project, this felt different. With my colleagues all elsewhere – taking with them the social expectations of a shared working environment – I began twice daily to visit the cheapest dessert shop for miles around, bringing my private shame back to the empty office, slurping luminous custard from a paper bowl or inhaling huge slices of what must be the most affordable by-the-slice chocolate gâteau in the whole of this unnamed, overpriced city.

Whenever I complained to my writer friends about my non-specific problems with the non-specific job, they told me to be thankful it wasn't worse. I heard stories of other writers in the industry, how all their attempts to pursue depth of character had been regarded with contempt. I spoke to a friend who spent a month writing three hundred different ways for Navy SEALs to say 'reload'.

I couldn't make myself feel lucky, though. I had the constant sense that the next small edit would balance the whole thing out, and I was always wrong. A branching story is like a creature with ten thousand limbs – if you tweak one toe, the whole thing convulses. Luckily, I got regular guidance from the game designers, for whom I have unending respect. These are people who can hold the multiverse in their heads. They would take a few hours to talk me through the shape of the story, the myriad directions in which players might travel and, for a few precious moments, I would understand exactly what I needed to do. Then the door shut behind them.

One day I heard that there was going to be a guided meditation class for staff at lunchtime, and I immediately signed up. We all gathered in the big meeting room. The focalizer was a young woman in a many-zipped black leather jacket that camouflaged her against the huge executive sofas on which we were all sitting. She dimmed the lights. We closed our eyes and she began to lead us down a long corridor in our minds. We had to choose one room opening off the corridor and go into it, finding a place where we could let go of our fears and worries. All of us were skipping lunch to be there and our stomachs creaked like the doors in horror films. As everyone entered their special place, I stayed in the corridor of possibility, knowing that, whichever room I chose, there would always be a better, more special room nearby. After a while, I opened my eyes and was relieved to find that one of my colleagues had opened her eyes too. We remained sitting in silence together, taking comfort in each other's failure, staring at the massive wall-mounted TV screen that hovered in the darkness like a portal.

Afterwards, as I was heading outside to get a sandwich, I happened to enter the lift at the same time as the focalizer. We smiled at each other awkwardly and she asked me how I'd found the session. It was a classic binary choice of the kind that gets used in branching narratives: I could either lie or confess. This is a useful dilemma in a game because, whatever the player chooses, it's easy for the situation to escalate. If the player opts to tell a friendly lie, then the person they're speaking to might see through it and confront them. If the player speaks the unfortunate truth, then the person might get upset or angry. In real life, I thanked her and told her that it had been amazing and she smiled and said she was glad to hear it. She said she could sense that we had really travelled somewhere. She was obviously lying and I was obviously lying and we were both hungry and waiting for the doors to open. The walls of the elevator were mirrored and we could see our more interesting selves multiplying into infinity.

Months later, when it was clear that the script was defeating me, the producers brought in a writer-director who had been nominated for a prize I shall not name. My colleagues asked me if I was willing to hand over the script so that the writer-director could help with 'final tweaks'. And in one branch of my life I stubbornly insisted on carrying my artistic vision through to completion, displaying the particular quality of arrogance that is associated with genius. And in another branch – the one I am living in – I handed over the script, half hoping that the writer-director would indeed find simple solutions to the problems I deemed insurmountable, half hoping that it would destroy their life. The writer-director said it might take them a couple of weeks. We waited. They were still working on it, they said. Almost there. Oh how I recognized that 'almost'. And then, one day months later, after a meeting in which my colleagues told me that the writer-director had stopped answering their phone, I was cycling home and happened to pass the writer-director in a garden square, surrounded by actors, back in their safe place: linear narrative.

Hard to blame them. I mean, I do blame them. But it is hard.

A few months later still, I got some news about the project. And in one branch of my life, the news was good and I am now heralded as the creative force behind what became a multi-award-winning interactive experience, one that has changed forever the way stories are told: my parents play it and, for the first time in their lives, they truly understand the power of the thing that robbed me of my childhood. And in the other branch – the branch I am writing from – the project I spent a year working on was axed and yet I will never be allowed to talk about it or use any of the material I wrote or even describe the story to anyone. In this branch, I try to ignore the noise from the other side of the wall: my happier self in his brand-new office chair, spinning, spinning, spinning.

DON'T THEY KNOW IT'S THE END OF THE WORLD? THE HELL OF *FALLOUT'S DEAD MONEY*

Lisa McInerney

I very quickly decided I didn't like 2015's *Fallout 4*. Even before the paucity of dialogue options was fully revealed, before the flop of a fight with the early-game Deathclaw in Concord, and before companion character Preston Garvey started wrecking my head by asking me to direct every stupid settler who couldn't figure out that crops needed water. I decided I didn't like *Fallout 4* as soon as I emerged from Vault 111 and saw how bright everything was. The sun was shining. The clouds were fluffy. My suit was a lurid blue. The Red Rocket truck stop was positively crimson. My God! I thought. What is this shiny happy nonsense? This is not my apocalypse!

Those who remain unfamiliar with the concept of *Fallout* are significantly less numerous than they used to be, given its well-received 2024 TV adaptation, but in short, it's a series of role-playing games – RPGs – built on the premise that devastating nuclear war broke out in 2077 between the United States and China, in the middle of a prolonged 1950s-coded golden age of America. Retrofuturism is the dilapidated look. Frozen hyper-nationalism is the backdrop. Settlements have risen, in a bockety way, from the ashes. There are so many interesting new drugs.

I am not an old-school *Fallout* player. At the time of their release, I was busy with *Super Mario 64* and the PlayStation era of *Final Fantasy* games: the fuzzy, awkwardly animated sprites and grungy environments of *Fallout*s *1* and *2* didn't grab me, and besides, I didn't own a PC. I started with *Fallout* on console: *Fallout 3* in 2008, the first of the series to be developed by Bethesda after they bought the rights to the franchise. It remains a pretty good game. It's set in the ruins of Washington, D.C. and follows the adventures of the Lone Wanderer, a young adult who leaves the safety of Vault 101 – the nuclear bunker where they grew up – to follow their father into the wastes. The exploration is fun, for the most part. The combat's fine. The father is voiced by Liam Neeson. He's holier-than-thou but at least you have the option to disappoint him by making monstrous decisions, like exploding thriving settlements or trading in slaves.

Fallout 3 was followed by what many fans consider the best game in the series – *Fallout: New Vegas*. Released in 2010, set in 2281, its story takes place in and around what's left of Las Vegas and the Mojave Desert. Your character is the Courier, ambushed, shot in the head and left for dead while carrying a mysterious package to the fortified and resurrected Las Vegas Strip. There's a power struggle underway between Mr House, custodian of the Strip and a huge number of very dangerous robots; the New Californian Republic, or NCR, who have an established military presence in the area and a problem with bureaucratic bloat; and Caesar's Legion, an army/cult presided over by an ex-Mormon who's really into Hegelian dialectics. The aesthetic is bone-dry and hot. The soundtrack is either diegetic mid-twentieth-century country and big band classics piped through on your radio, or non-diegetic forlorn instrumentals. 'Patrolling the Mojave almost makes you wish for a nuclear winter,' bemoan sundry NCR grunts, trudging past stubbornly surviving cacti and mutated cattle (there are worse mutated things in the Mojave, and you won't be trudging past any of them). *Fallout: New Vegas* (or, simply, *FNV*) is a compelling adventure, offering multiple paths through its narrative and in which no good deed goes unpunished. It has four main add-on narratives in the form of downloadable content (DLC), all with different flavours, that reveal more of the Courier's backstory and confront us with new adversaries. My favourite of these add-ons is *Dead Money*.

It is still somewhat controversial in the *Fallout* community to say your favourite of these add-ons is *Dead Money*.

I learned about the end of the world in my local library. It was the 1990s, and the end of the world wasn't even in fashion anymore, but my local library was well-worn, and its children's section dotted with books published during the Cold War. I was a greedy reader and even then liked my books unsettling; I was the kind of child who'd hole up reading woe-betides about drug addiction in *Reader's Digest*, or serial killer biographies in sensational true crime magazines I'd nick from older relatives. It was in our little library I unearthed books like Robert C. O'Brien's *Z for Zachariah*, published in 1974, and Louise Lawrence's *Children of the Dust*, from 1985. There were others, but these two stuck with me. The imagery in both was potent and brazenly grim: the radiation suit and the awful trek into the unknown in *Z for Zachariah*; the fallout infiltrating through a forgotten chimney in *Children of the Dust*, radiation sickness wreaking havoc on the children's bodies. Preparation, in a way, for my eventually watching *Threads*, the 1984 BBC film depicting nuclear annihilation as experienced by an ordinary young couple in Sheffield, expecting their first baby. Here too were scenes proving personally and unfortunately indelible. I'm not going to list them. If you've seen *Threads* you know them, and if you haven't seen *Threads* it's not my place to inflict *Threads* on you. The point being that as far as I'm concerned there's an apocalyptic aesthetic and it's sacred. It should feel heartbreaking and breathtaking. It should feel eschatological and Blakean, as befitting the sharpest edge to religious thought, which in itself is frightening. It should be grand and dark and patterned and wrong. It should, above all else, feel lonely.

Loneliness is bad. This we all know. In minor or fleeting form it makes us sad, stresses us, attacks our self-esteem. When chronic, it leaves us susceptible to a suite of physical and mental illnesses. It's only recently begun to be treated as a significant public health issue, despite its cohering with sensory deprivation, which when extended or involuntary is torturous (as proven by the experiments of Donald O. Hebb or Harry Harlow). Many who've experienced solitary confinement, for example, stress that they wouldn't wish it on their worst enemy. The effects of solitary confinement – in which a person is not only segregated but deprived of mental and physical stimulation – include but are not limited to anxiety, depression, paranoia, psychosis, self-harm, hallucinations, obsessive thoughts, high blood pressure, headaches, irregular heartbeat and permanent alteration to brain physiology.

Writers of horror media have long made use of our innate dread of loneliness. At the end of *Z for Zachariah*, Anne leaves as her antagonist, unable to follow, begs her to stay; Sarah in *Children of the Dust* must find a home for her little sister before she takes her own life; Ruth in *Threads* is subjected to the loss of everyone she loves and any semblance of positive social connection by the breakdown of her country. Beyond the post-apocalyptic, think of the geographical isolation and the whittling down of the research station's already tiny human population in John Carpenter's *The Thing*; the social isolation of both

Joe and Matt in *Black Mirror*'s *White Christmas*; or the mere concept of an oubliette, a narrow, vertical dungeon in medieval castles where prisoners were said to have been abandoned (*oublier* meaning 'to forget', though it should be noted that there's no convincing evidence of an oubliette being used for its assumed purpose, and that they were probably just drainage holes, but the idea of it is horrible and we don't want the truth to get in the way of a skin-crawling scare).

There are plenty of examples from my favourite video games. Some of the non-lethal mission solutions in the *Dishonored* games – which could be described as pre-apocalyptic, depending on how you choose to play – invoke the horror of pure isolation so effectively, they cannot be classed as benevolent actions. In one, a witch is tricked into transferring her consciousness to the Void, a limitless, timeless dimension, where she must exist in a state of fragmented nothingness. In another, the corrupt head of a militant religious faction can be branded a heretic and cast out from everything he knows; providing any comfort or assistance to him is forbidden. The *Elder Scrolls* series has a few nasty examples. A wizard in *Oblivion* is cursed to an endless, solitary nightmare for stealing from a dark god; in *Skyrim* you must visit the Soul Cairn, a desolate spirit plane where enslaved souls are doomed to roam, confused and frightened, for eternity. Your investigation in *Disco Elysium* leads you to an elderly suspect shattered by shame and self-imposed isolation, his political cause long forgotten by everyone except him. The ending of my own favourite game, *Final Fantasy VIII*, has

Squall, its introvert protagonist, lost in time, in a barren, dark nightmare, utterly alone. Incidentally, he's rescued by the girl he loves, a sorceress far more powerful than he is, which I find very refreshing.

What makes the horror of loneliness especially effective in video games is the suggestion of complicity; 'suggestion', because of course video games are still scripted, and your agency as a player is massively oversold if it exists at all. That you may have brought your character to this end is one source of discomfort; that you are meant to experience this with them is another. Action's consequence is the driving force of narrative. Some of the consequences of your actions, as in the *Dishonored* non-lethal paths, may dawn on you much later, and make you feel very queasy; this is what makes them good examples of 'fridge horror', a term related to the 'icebox scene' theory often attributed to Hitchcock (a scene whose implications hit you hours later, when you've left the cinema and are rummaging for chicken in the icebox). Some consequences are those you have to play through, by which I mean sort of live through vicariously; this is where your character finds themself and you must manoeuvre them out again. *Skyrim*'s Soul Cairn is a godforsaken place to be even if you're in actuality sitting on the couch in your pyjamas. Consequence is a reality you've made. Complicity is the capsaicin in your chilli.

The *Fallout* series is very good at suggesting the horror of loneliness. The vaults themselves – the bunkers where most of the series' protagonists begin – are isolated and sealed. They're home to claustrophobic, paranoid mini societies when populated, and are no more than eerie tombs once breached, decaying testaments to exploitation or hubris or corruption. The atmosphere, then, of *Dead Money* shouldn't be so unusual in the context of the wider *Fallout* franchise, and yet in its relentlessness, its commitment to the lost and lonesome, it is.

Dead Money is set in the Sierra Madre, an opulent casino which was about to celebrate its grand opening gala when the Great War bombs fell. Its security systems activated, sealing it off from the world; no one could get in, and no one could get out. As the years went by, the casino's degrading climate control system released a lethal toxic cloud that hovered over and preserved the Sierra Madre and the Villa, the residential neighbourhoods surrounding it. The Villa's streets are home to the 'Ghost People', the silent, mutated remnants of the maintenance workers sealed in their Hazmat suits when the bombs fell, 200 years before. The Courier – your character – is lured to a strange bunker by a pre-war broadcast advertising the Sierra Madre's opening gala event, where they are knocked out and transported to the Villa. You wake wearing an explosive collar. You've been enslaved by a mysterious figure named Father Elijah, and are tasked with finding the three other souls he's stuck explosive collars on. Once together, you'll be instructed to trigger the gala event, which will open the casino doors; from there, Elijah intends to crack the Sierra Madre vault, said to contain the treasure of pre-war America. Unless you're able to get there before him. It would, the game tells you, be the heist of the centuries.

So far, so fun. You'll have done this before in *FNV*. Go here, get information, bring it back to the quest-giver. Go there, press a button, trigger a scene. But it quickly becomes apparent that this is not your typical *FNV* environment. The Villa streets are choked with that toxic cloud, dense pockets of which will ravage your health in seconds; everything has a dirty red tinge. What little you see of the sky is burnt and static. The buildings are dark and crumbling. There are hologram vendors here and there, generic, invulnerable, silent; interacting with them results in the same melancholy line: 'The flickering hologram stares at you expectantly'. There is no comforting sound: no friendly radio stations to listen to, no secondary characters to chat to as you explore, no shopkeepers, no coyote's wail along the trail. And in the way that a slight invocation of what you're missing makes the longing worse, the other characters you must recruit for Elijah's scheme are damaged: one is psychologically disturbed, another is bitter and duplicitous, the third has been mutilated to the point of losing her voice. Each must be enlisted, then either vanquished or abandoned in pursuit of Elijah and access to the vault. No fellowship, this. Assuming you're able to trigger the gala event and unlock the casino – while jaunty swing music plays over an ominous looping hum that must be heard to be believed, and Ghost People swarm towards you – what awaits inside provides relief for mere minutes.

If the Villa is a monument to hubris, the Sierra Madre is a monument to paranoia. It is perfectly preserved and quiet as the grave. It's patrolled by mute security holograms who shoot to kill. It's staffed by hologram croupiers and bartenders, none of whom can do much beyond flicker noiselessly. Underline the dead in *Dead Money*.

No, the Sierra Madre isn't a mere casino; it's a fortress, built by businessman Frederick Sinclair for the starlet Vera Keyes, with whom he was deeply in love. Seeing war on the horizon, Sinclair threw everything into the casino's construction, making terrible alliances in a bid to keep Vera safe. But Vera had her own secrets. Blackmailed by Rat Pack-style sleazebag Dean Domino, she was the reluctant key to a scheme to ransack the vault. Sinclair, aware of Dean's intentions, had covertly transformed the vault from a shelter to a trap (there's even a 'Cask of Amontillado' reference). Wretched with guilt, Vera confessed to Sinclair, who realized he couldn't condemn the woman he loved to such a lonely death. But then the bombs fell.

Sinclair died trying to undo the terrible modifications he'd made. The Sierra Madre shut itself up as intended. Its security holograms massacred the guests. Vera was trapped in her room and took her own life. Dean was 'ghoulified' – mutated rather than killed by the radiation, and cursed with an extended lifespan – while his obsession with his planned heist tethered him to the Sierra Madre and he watched over it, stuck in an undead body, alone. The distress beacon malfunctioned, replaced by a looped recording of Vera inviting those wanting to 'begin again' to the casino's grand opening – the same broadcast the Courier responds to, 200 years later.

Dead Money ends with a showdown with Father Elijah, who, you discover, is motivated by much worse than treasure. What he wants is to 'wipe the slate clean. Make the Mojave like it was meant to be: undisturbed by man. I'll send the Cloud, the Holograms...' With new urgency, you can either kill Elijah or lure him into the vault and trap him there, assuming you don't manage to trap yourself in the vault, which is very possible if you let greed get the better of you. The treasure is, in the context of the game, more than worth it: 37 gold bars worth almost 400,000 caps (in-game currency). The bad news is that each bar weighs 35 pounds, so the chances of your Courier being able to make off with more than one or two are slim. This is assuming you don't painstakingly manipulate the game mechanics or use cheats, and you shouldn't, because that'd break the moral of the story.

Is there a worse way to die? Sealed into a tomb, surrounded by the treasure of a world long gone, with no chance of rescue because nobody knows where you are, in the heart of a city of the dead, in the middle of a lethal wilderness. Trapping Elijah in the vault is momentarily satisfying, but there is no 'good' ending to *Dead Money*. Even if they're still alive, you never see your companions again. You cannot return to the casino, or the Villa around it. You leave empty-handed... or you don't leave at all.

Fallout: New Vegas should not be played without incorporating its DLCs, which add so much lore, and so much context for the Courier's journey. *Old World Blues* is probably the fans' darling, modelled on cheesy 1950s B movies. *Honest Hearts*, set in Zion National Park, serves as an oasis in all that urban hell. *Lonesome Road* is foreboding, though not all that lonesome: the Courier walks towards their defining confrontation, mostly alone, but in (kind of interminable) dialogue with their nemesis. *Dead Money* is survival horror riveted onto an open-world adventure; its difficulty spike and drastic change of tone and pace still provokes ire in a significant portion of *FNV* fans. It feels like you've been dropped into a different game.

This is the reason I love *Dead Money*. It is so instantly unsettling, so unapologetically difficult. When your Courier wakes up in that explosive collar in the grounds of the Villa, they realize that all of their equipment is missing: their weapons, medicine, food, armour. There are very limited weapons to be found, and they may not suit your Courier's carefully developed skill set. All that's learned must be reimagined. And there is nothing to soften the blow, no suggestion of possible one-upmanship, nowhere to rest and take stock. You are, the game coldly stresses, *on your own*.

When I was small, I had this recurring nightmare. It was completely dark. There was no impression of my even having eyes, or a body at all. I was a consciousness in a void, anticipating… something. Some precise moment I had no foreknowledge of; I would know it when it came, and I could not afford to miss it, because if I did I would be doomed to remain in the void. And of course I always missed it, and I would know I was stuck there in this emptiness for a cycle of incredible duration. I would wake up screaming.

I had other nightmares without visuals, too. A feeling of something crumpling, something which could not be put right again. I stopped having these nightmares before I hit my teens, and I don't tend to dream without visuals anymore, thankfully. I had other kinds of nightmares as a child, of course, your common-or-garden bogeyman chasing me as my legs moved as if through soup, but what made those blind nightmares so terrifying was that there were no other entities there with me. Far worse than being pursued and endangered was the feeling of being totally alone. It was just me, innocent but ageless, insignificant, in the abyss.

The definition of Hell with which we're probably all most familiar is that of an afterlife in which sinners are subjected to punishment and torture and from which there is no escape. The manner of that torture has been subject to interpretation and reinterpretation by religious authorities, but in nearly all cases, damnation is self-imposed and characterized by isolation from God, from goodness and fraternity and joy. There are plenty of lakes of fire and brimstone and all of that, but modern interpretations lean away from the literal. Hell is fucking yourself over. It manifests only at the end of all things. Hell is what's left when there's nothing left… Hell should, above all else, feel *lonely*.

Dead Money's moral was carefully crafted. The hard part, the game tells you, isn't getting to the Sierra Madre. The hard part is *letting go*. But letting go of what? All of that lovely gold? Well yeah, this is the simplest reading of it – you bleed for the treasure but then you can't take it with you. As in life, we suffer to accumulate *things* and then we die. But there's more to it. We're letting go of something other than the Sierra Madre's treasure. 'Let Go', Vera's last words, are scrawled on the wall of her room – a message to Sinclair, pleading with him to abandon his quest, for nothing matters now? Or a final understanding of her predicament: abandon hope? In *Dead Money* we're directed to let go of the past, which in *Fallout*'s context means the before-times, the pre-apocalypse, the glamour, the golden age, the retrofuturism, the horribly preserved hope. We must see it for what it is: utter failure. The fumbling of the moment the tide might have turned. And in Elijah, we get a perfect representation of true madness: the man who craves and pursues isolation, looks to inflict it on himself. 'I'll kill them until it's only me,' he says, 'me alone in a quiet world.' *Dead Money* doesn't ask us to reject gold bars. *Dead Money* asks us to acknowledge the abyss.

Complicity, in video games, is either constructed or simulated. Even in open-world RPGs like those of the *Fallout* series, your choices are limited to those the writers have devised for you. We know this, and as gamers we accept this; the skilful illusion of choice is all we need, and we know that we are not truly complicit, that it's all a glamour. Again, complicity equates in this context with agency, itself simulated; the draw of the interactive narrative is that you can, on some level, feel like you're experiencing it first-hand. The idea, then, with games that devise hells for us to play through is that it allows us to explore the dark in safety – the literal dark, as in *Dead*

Money's corroded streets, or the metaphorical dark, soul-darkness, as in *Dead Money*'s broken characters, suffering ambition that will do nothing but hollow them out. But more again: experiencing loneliness second-hand moves us to sympathy. There's no fantasy in trauma so human; this isn't like mourning teammates after a high-octane ambush in a first-person shooter, or wallowing in the righteousness of revenge, macho violence masquerading as trauma. Exploring loneliness, directing a character through a barren landscape, is a homage to connection. And though it would be a stretch to call *Dead Money* transgressive, it does what all great transgressive fictions do: allows us space to feel and to fear, to switch the light off and stare into the mirror. How better to explore what it means to be alive than be surrounded by all of life's antitheses?

A few years ago, while in Madrid's Museo del Prado, I saw Francisco Goya's Black Paintings. These are a collection of fourteen bleak murals Goya created on the walls of his house, reflecting his developing misanthropy, his fear of madness, his dwindling hope. *Saturn Devouring his Son*, that's one of them, kind of a meme now because sometimes there's nothing to do with horror but giggle uneasily at it; in real life it is fucking unnerving. You may also bring to mind *The Dog*, which depicts a half-sunken pup, mournful and near-lost in the vastness of the painting. Perhaps *The Fates*, those crones floating horribly over a murky landscape? I was profoundly moved by the Black Paintings. They're huge, for a start, exquisitely oppressive. It feels wrong to speak in their presence. It's likely Goya never wanted them to be publicly displayed: they were for him only, they depict loneliness, they substantiate loneliness. They confirm that there's creativity in despair. They are the most beautiful things I've ever seen in my life.

I am not making the argument that *Dead Money* is equivalent to the Black Paintings, though I do believe that *Dead Money* is the strongest component of *Fallout: New Vegas*, a truly great video game. I think that, in its way, *Dead Money* pushes us to define what we feel when we're confronted by bald despair, that it feels like an active inspection of what the Black Paintings represent. It is horror that we can poke about in and take our time with, should we feel up to it. What is the end of the world, really? What does it mean to find yourself in Hell? It seems to me that it's what's left when everything else is taken from you. Community, initiative, lungfuls of air, birdsong, fluffy clouds, blue sky, crimson paint. All that remains is all that you are. And because you do not want to imagine it, you must imagine it.

TIP OF MY JOYSTICK

Sheila Armstrong

This is a forum for finding the name of a game that you can't remember. Read the rules, post your description, and hopefully someone will be able to identify it. To help us, please provide as much information as possible, including:

- keywords
- platform
- estimated year of release
- genre
- art style
- gameplay mechanics
- characters

Be sure to help out if you think you may have an answer to someone else's post![1]

---

[1] r/tipofmyjoystick

Passenger Seat / PlayStation 1 & SNES / 1996

In this game, you have no consoles in your house, so you have to sneak across to your boy-cousins' to watch them play. Over their shoulders, you learn how to take down an AT-AT with a tow cable[1] and the precise cadence of Get Over Here.[2] In the playground, no other child can do Sonic's impatient foot taps[3] as well as you.

Late at night, you watch the boys play flash games from the depths of the early internet: Columbine-style massacres with fountains of blood and decapitated teachers; the hoover from Teletubbies giving blow-jobs; a paedophilic Bear in the Big Blue House armed with a shotgun.[4] They never let you hold the controller, sit at the keyboard, wrap your tiny fingers around the joystick.

As an adult, you discover playthroughs and fall asleep to strangers talking to themselves like children over Lego. You worry that this over-the-shoulder position has done long-term psychological damage. You are less worried about the decapitations and blow-jobs.

---

1 <Ehhh… this could be any of a few *Star Wars* games. It's like a staple at this stage. *Shadows of the Empire?*>

2 <Could have been either *MK 3* or *4* if it was late 1990s.>

3 <Megadrive *Sonic*, Genesis in the US.>

4 <These were all Newgrounds flash games made by Tom Fulp. Weird guy.>

The Most Important Meal of the Day / PC / 1999

This game arrives on a disc in your cereal box. Your parents don't like video games, but capitalism gives you this one for free. You play as one of three trademarked characters: the tiger can jump, the monkey can swing from trees and the doughy-faced elf can swim. You leap around a primary-coloured landscape, fighting off crocodiles who have stolen your nutritious breakfast cereal.[1]

An overzealous substitute teacher gives you a punishment: write a day in the life of a Rice Krispie. You write a story about Snap, Crackle and Pop, vicious capitalist dictators ruling over hordes of servile rice field workers; grains ripped from families, the gnashing and moaning of teeth. This is all very funny, until you have to read it out to the class, which is when it becomes not funny at all, and you realize what the real punishment was all along – to listen to the sound of your own voice.

Your light-speed, shameful stutters are overlaid with the rising panic of the music as the snorkelling elf runs out of air. You always get stuck on underwater levels. You imagine what is just beyond the water: boss battles, flame-throwers, power-ups; entire kingdoms to claim.

American soldiers painted Snap, Crackle and Pop on the noses of World War II bombers: delivery with a smile. In Vietnam, choppers bore Snoopy the Sniper and

---

1 <I know this one – Kellogg's *Mission Nutrition*!!! I still have my Nordic-language copy from when I was seven. Can't even get it to run on a Win 95 emulator though. Trust me, I spent a whole day trying.>

blondes in fishnets; now, heavy metal singers sign bombs for Gaza with a flourish.

When your brother chooses the name of his new boat, it is a careful, thoughtful process. He ignores the obvious puns (Fishin' Impossible, Breaking Wind, Happy Oar) and settles on *Éadáil*, sea-Irish from Árainn Mhór that means flotsam, wreckage, spoils. His friend paints the name on the transom, and afterwards writes a careful, loving account of each whisk of sandpaper, each curve of the grain, each flick of the synthetic-sable brush.

(Don't Wanna Be Your) Monkey Wrench / PC / 2000

after point and click adventure games

In this game, you combine random, illogical items to solve undecipherable puzzles. This sort of angular thinking gives you nothing except a life-long addiction to puns and a tendency to attack your inventory like a college student facing a bare cupboard.

Problem: A waterfall is blocking a secret passage.

    Solution: Get arrested and thrown in jail. USE a stick to flip a dead prisoner's femur towards you. GIVE bone to dog in exchange for the keys. PICK UP a guerilla envelope on your way out. OPEN envelope to find a banana. FIND a piano-playing monkey. USE the banana with the metronome. PICK UP hypnotized monkey. USE stiff monkey on water pump to turn off waterfall and reveal passage. WHAT the hell.[1]

Problem: A dragon requires six golden trinkets for its hoard.

    Solution: LOOK AT fishmonger's shiny belt bucket. USE string to tie up octopus. PUT octopus in outhouse bucket. FEED custard to octopus. ADD prunes to caviar. WATCH fishmonger eat spiked caviar and run to outhouse. WATCH fishmonger be sexually assaulted by octopus. STEAL gold belt buckle. CURSE Eric Idle for

---

1 <*Monkey Island 2.* Had never heard the term monkey wrench before, so I was confused even when I solved it.>

being involved in this mess of a game. WONDER what the custard was for.[2]

Problem: An underground rebel movement needs eggs to train a fleet of carrier pigeons.

Solution: TAKE balloon shaped like Robert Frost from angry clown. CLIMB makeshift rope to roof of Department of Death. Approach skeletal pigeons. SHAKE Robert Frost Balloon at skeletal pigeons. LISTEN to your character: 'Run you pigeons, it's Robert Frost!' WAIT while nothing happens. Rage QUIT. WAIT fifteen years. FIND walkthrough.

The bread of the dead is a standard loaf of Cuban bread. The bread is obtained from a stall at the El Marrow festival and used as a means of attracting the rooftop pigeons. After crumbling it into the dish on the rooftop alongside the Robert Frost Balloon, the pigeon's pecking will cause the balloon to explode and scare them off, allowing Manny to retrieve their eggs.

FUCK this game.[3]

---

2 <*Discworld.* These 1990s puzzle games were on another level. Never finished it.>
3 <Ugh. *Grim Fandango.* I had no idea who Robert Frost was either.>

↑ ↑ ↓ ↓ ← → ← → A-C-A-B / PC / 2001

This game belongs to another cousin, handed off like an old sock. You play as a woman, and that's cool – you always want to play as a woman – and she's black, with an apostrophe in her name, which is extra cool; you don't know any black people yet, but more than that, she's American and you still don't think America is a real place. Your fists are spheres because fingers are hard to animate, and you move like a reskinned Lara Croft, which you probably are, and you can do a side kick so high it looks like your leg will break off.

It's raining in the washed-out city, with smashed windows and burnt-out cars, and an eerie chime in a minor key rings out every few minutes. Cops are bumbling and corrupt (and Irish; even now you know you're the butt of the joke, without knowing exactly what the joke is) and you're the new recruit. There are three types of NPCs: people in suits and gangbangers and prostitutes, and as the cows grumble outside your window, you imagine that's what all cities are like. You can arrest people – All Cops Are Bastards of course, but you are less so: you help suicidal jumpers down from buildings and catch muggers and blow up drug caches – but you can also use shotguns and baseball bats and grenades to mow down anyone who gets in your way. The AK-47 is your favourite.

You fire one, in real life, outside the Killing Fields of Cambodia, in a place geared towards slug-hungry tourists. You look at boxes full of teeth, children's teeth, and learn that the Khmer Rouge didn't waste bullets on babies, but instead smashed their heads off a particular tree, that they put speakers in that tree and played music to drown out the executions. But none of that matters, because firing an AK-47 feels *good*: you are D'arci Stern and those gangbangers are falling in a particularly satisfying way – their legs are whipped backwards from under them and they land face down in a pool of their own blood.

Babies probably don't have that much blood.

The final boss was a cult leader, or a warlock; there was also a balrog, for some reason.[1] Decades later, you find out it was a runner-up for GameSpot's Worst Game of 2000. Your heart breaks a little for D'arci Stern, but all the voice actresses listed on the IMDB page are blonde and white.

---

1 <Was it *Urban Chaos*? That game was great, but had a wild ending. One of the first proper open worlds before *GTA*. And the first game to have a black female MC!>

No Gods Or Kings / Xbox / 2008

You lie on the couch to play this game and lazily wonder whether to blow up a town built around an atomic bomb, for 1,000 caps and minus 1,000 karma points.[1] Your companion is a Blue Heeler called Dogmeat, and you don't want to disappoint him. The boogie-woogie 1950s soundtrack pairs nicely with the Bloody Mess perk as your enemies explode into gore. It's the Atomic Age, baby: America is on the up-up-up, and retrofuturism is all the rage.

In Fritz Lang's sci-fi dystopia *Metropolis* (1927), camera angles slash stark shadows across sharp-edged buildings. Wealthy industrialists lounge above a mechanical city powered by brutalized workers, so desperate for a messiah they destroy their own homes. The actors are pale and doughy, while the metal skin of the *maschinenmensch*, the robot-human, is as flimsy as the film's message: *Mittler zwischen Hirn und Händen muss das Herz sein* – the mediator between the head and the hands must be the heart.

You enjoy a good morality system, in theory. In practice, you always choose a knock-out strangle over a knife to the throat and watch the bad ending later on YouTube. You're under no illusions that this makes you a good person: the Low Chaos option is often worse than the High.[2] You hold a dead empress's heart in your hands as

---

1 <It's mentioned in *New Vegas* and *4*, but the Megaton quest was *Fallout 3*.>
2 < In the first *Dishonored*, you can give a woman to her stalker instead of killing her, and in *D2* you can electrocute a genius back into the Stone Age. Objectively more evil than just murdering them outright.>

you ghost through a Victorian steampunk city and it whispers dirty little secrets to you. In an underwater Art Deco city, little sisters see corpses as angels: a man chooses, a slave obeys.[3] In an Irrational city, seething disorganization and employee PTSD under an indecisive boss: mandatory crunch and twelve-hour days. In a Brutalist cardboard city, child extras from the poorest districts of Berlin work for weeks in a pool of cold water, while Fritz Lang hurls his extras into violent mob scenes, his lead actress into the heat of real flames.

Retrofuturism – that old, dry-tongued hope for an elevated future – only ever tastes like disappointment.

The hands holding the controller consult with the head and the heart. You save your game and choose both options: set off the bomb, then disarm it. Before you press the ignition switch, you press F to toggle between first-person and third-person point of view. The difference is unsettling.

---

3 <This sounded so profound when I was twelve, but your choices don't really matter in the end. Ken Levine treats his developers like shit too. I almost hope *Bioshock 4* doesn't happen.>

Head, Shoulders, Knees & Toes / Browser / 2010

Instead of writing your college essays, you become obsessed with a silly, impossible game that people forward to their friends. Q and W control the right and left thighs, O and P control the calves. The game plays as if you are an alien puppeteering a human for the first time. Inspirational music swells when you step forward, cutting out with a crunch as your athlete collapses into a mess of limbs. If you somehow manage to reach the halfway point, a hurdle appears that you must jump, or, more likely, barrel through and hope it doesn't tangle in your feet. At the 100-metre mark, a sandpit appears: your final task is to leap, un-gazelle-like, and become a long-jump national hero.[1]

As existential crises go, the simulation hypothesis is only a six out of ten: enough for a quarter hour of horror, maybe a mildly restless night. Any souped-up descendants running the simulation of their ancestors are either there, or they are not. If they are there, they are horribly disappointed that this is how you spend your time.

Finally, you crack it: you tip backwards so your back leg is bent, knee to the ground, and your front leg waves ahead of you like a fleshy white cane. You twitch and spasm the full 100 metres to the finish line. Your leap is 0.1 of a metre.

---

1 *<QWOP*. So addictive. Used to play this all the time while stoned, lol.>

It's About Ethics in Video Games Journalism, Actually / PC / 2015

> Once upon a time, a woman decided what
> she wanted most in the world was to
> become a video game designer.

Your boyfriend sets up your account and leaves you to play this game while he goes to college: undead, a hunter, with a purple wolf by your side. Do you…

1. Play for a few minutes and get bored.
2. Play for six hours and don't hear him coming home.

> The woman grew up and made
> a choose-your-own-adventure game about
> her depression.[1]

Many quests later, a network glitch means you have to start over with a new character every time you boot the game up. Do you…

1. Play every single combination of race and class, restarting over and over, without ever leaving the starting area.
2. Type /played into the search bar and realize you are wasting your life.

> A games journalist wrote a review of the
> video game. The woman's ex-boyfriend

---

1 <*Depression Quest*. Google the Quinnspiracy. Not saying any more or I'll get banned.>

> disliked this. The ex-boyfriend wrote that
> the woman had fucked the journalist for
> the review.

A friend will invite you on a raid, and you will embarrass him, because it turns out you haven't been playing the right way at all. You'll realize two things then: one is that you're bad at games – really bad – and the second is that men hate you. They hate that you're bad, and they hate that you're there at all: they just hate you. You begin to learn then that you won't be the exception, that there is no such thing as not like other girls. You dress up as a Jill Sandwich for Halloween, and men quiz you on trivia in smoking areas. Do you:

1. Get thicker skin and learn how to raid properly.
2. Play all the way to level 85 by yourself, grinding slow.[2]

> The internet didn't like the ex-boyfriend's
> story. The internet didn't like that at all.
> The internet didn't like women at all. The
> internet thought politics was destroying
> their favourite games.

You cackle while wielding a chainsaw, facing down a charger zombie,[3] and you sense a soft, strange thing: the feeling of someone falling in love with you. He collects

---

2 <If the cap was 85 it was *Cataclysm*.>
3 <Chargers were L4D2. Absolute units.>

consoles: you are paralysed by choice. He builds you a gaming PC from spare parts and you play and play and play. You occasionally persuade him to sit with you in front of a multiplayer, but he gets frustrated with you every time. Do you…

1. Stay for another few years.
2. Step into the unknown.

> The internet found the women's addresses. The internet threatened to blow them up, to shoot them in the head, to strangle their pets. The internet sent the women drawings of themselves being raped by video game characters.[4]

He comes home from work and straight into a game about rocket-powered cars, leaning into the keyboard as if he is a baby with a driving wheel toy.[5] You know by the force of the clack if he is swerving, firing, scoring a point. You know another little sound too, the guilty-backslide of his gaming chair when you get up to do the dishes again. Do you…

1. Say it.
2. Wait for him to say it.

> Why are women always so sensitive?

---

4 <I don't condone it, but Wu was a real bitch at the time. Do you remember the Beat Up Anita Sarkeesian flash game? Guilty pleasure>

5 <R-r-r-r-rooocckkkettt Leeeaaaguueee>

At the end of all things, he'll cry in a way you've only seen twice before. Once was when he sat for half an hour at the end of his favourite game (*Part II*), unable to press the final button, end the final fight. He'll take all your (his) consoles with him, and you'll play nothing for a long, long time.

Noclip mode / PS4 / 2020

This game is alone in your room, but you don't feel alone, because millions of others are alone in their rooms too. Fast travel is the gaming mechanic you've most often envied. Blinking to friends or family on different continents, browsing the Amazon rainforest, then sleeping in your own bed. Circumstances have kept you anchored to one city, but the iron cuff is of your own making. You seek out every quest, every question mark, every blank patch of map, every scrap of lore.

> A map stretches, intensifies, emphasizes; it prefers
> simple to complex, straight lines to curved.

You write a novel to keep yourself sane but go mad in the process. Strangers read it and tell you what your characters and settings look like. You struggle to visualize things: spatial descriptions have always been useless to you. You cannot picture an apple. You open the HUD and close it again, open and close. Right or left at the fork?

> A map is an assertion of power, the
> enforcement of a cartographer's eye.

The border between Haafingar and Whiterun,[1] Crow's Perch and Crookback Bog,[2] may be long-disputed, skirmishes pushing it west or east by a metre or a mile, but on

---

[1] <*Skyrim*, obviously. It only sold 60 million copies… eye roll.>

[2] <Why are people using this forum instead of Google? You'd get *The Witcher 3* in 2 seconds, max.>

the map it is a single clean brushstroke. A toddler-scrawled executive order changes the name of a Gulf, and cowards fall in line.

A map is time and outside time.

You skim, wraith-like, through deserted video game levels, clipping through walls and floors without flinching.[3] Haunted mansions, dark realms, bone caverns, potion shops, fairground rides: without NPCs or a soundtrack, they are deathly still, frozen, little bulbil-shaped universes. Planted, a bulbil will grow into a genetic clone of the parent plant, but the laziest interpretation of the multiverse tells us that anything that can happen, will happen, must happen.

A map is a shared fantasy, superimposed on topography.

The elves believe troublesome humans arrived in the first Conjunction of the Spheres, when overlapping worlds collided and mingled. That is their story; the humans tell another, as they sit in their millions, alone in their rooms. Cartographers used to leave trap streets, phantom settlements, invented islands on their maps as a trademark. In south-central Finland, there is a small body of water called Onpahanvaanlampi; it translates to the

---

3 Noclip.website

sigh of a bored local to a passing cartographer: 'It's just a pond.'

A map tells white lies.

Afterwards, you listen to a playlist called Traveller's Rest on buses through twisting passes in northern Spain, crossing the Outback in a Land Rover, circling over a regional Indonesian airport. A compilation of music from open-world games, it transforms the passing landscape into an RPG, your movements into an epic quest. Right or left has never mattered, as long as you move.

Lemmingology / Floppy disc / 2024

This game introduces you to the concept of suicide in 16 bits. The green and purple sprites are indistinct, but still you assign them expressions and complex personalities. You are sad when you have to sacrifice one for the sake of the others; you try jumping off high things with an umbrella to slow your downward drift.

In 1958, Disney's eco-documentary *White Wilderness* followed a troupe of lemmings in the Canadian tundra. The footage is stark: tiny bodies tumble from a cliff, feet over paws. They try to stop themselves, climb back up; their legs skid in the dry earth, creating tiny avalanches. Goofy, bumbling music plays in the background, as if they are soft-edged animations rather than terrified rodents. They plop into the water like little heart attacks and swim out to sea. The stiff voiceover tells us that they will drown: 'The lemmings consider this body of water just another lake.' You try to explain to a friend that the urge to die can be both passive and constant, an in-built character skill.

Skills[1]	Action
Walker	You leave the Berlin State Library after another day of restless words.
Builder	Outside, someone has placed a series of stickers on an electricity box. The familiar sprites climb in single file: green hair and blue smocks; pale, pixelated limbs.
Blocker	Beyond the library, the Polizei make a wall with their bodies.
Basher	A woman wails over the slaughter, her 16-bit scarf patterned black and white. A dead-eyed Aryan officer forces her face into the ground and kneels on her neck.
Miner	You want to break through and help her.
Bomber	You want everyone and everything to stop and pay attention.
	Instead, you walk back and forth, back and forth, back and forth, hoping someone assigns you a role.

---

1 <These were the skills in the original game. This messed me up as a child. I thought you were helping the lemmings get somewhere nice!! Not leading them to a horrible death...>

The 1959 Academy Award for Best Documentary goes to *White Wilderness*. Decades later, the camera crew admit to paying kids 25 cents to round up some lemmings and drive them to Canada. They jostle them on snow-covered turntables and invisible hands shove them, dizzy, off a cliff; they fall through a trapdoor, down onto your screen.

At the end of each level, beyond the final door, the sky is blue. 'And if it's just another lake, it must have a farther shore.'

Android's Dream / 2077

In this game, each person who passes you is the result of a randomized character creator. Pink Mario pipes drape the streets, siphoning water out of the swamp the city is built on; the engineers chose pink because very young boys and girls both claim it as their favourite colour.

Outside the U-Bahn station, an artist sells planks of wood, graffiti styled in splattered vomits of paint.

BLOWJOBS 4 THE HOMELESS

CUM / PISS / FUCK

CUNT 4 president

vegans FUCK better

On trains, you play back your own braindances, but only the bad ones.[1] There are other, better memories you could choose to experience in 4D – a lusty day in the life of a pop star, the dead wind of a lunar skydive – but you have one genre bookmarked, and it is Shame.

In the Computerspielemuseum, you walk in circles, uncomfortable. You want to open your trench coat to show off your credentials: button masher, hack 'n' slasher, rage-quitter, save-scummer. You know how to get the rocket launcher car, the endless coin, the mother-lode, the exploding sheep, the bloody fatalities.

---

1 <They added more braindances in the *Phantom Liberty* DLC, but they're just vendor junk that you can't actually play. Such a cool concept, if developers had bothered following through.>

In the back of the museum, there is a room full of booths, each fitted with a console and décor from another decade. You can sit in a low-slung padded sofa and play *Pong* amongst the earth tones and wood panelling of the 1970s. In the 1980s room, the NES sits under a *Return of the Jedi* poster and copies of *Mad* magazine. Black leather beanbags, a plastic CD tower and a PlayStation set the 1990s scene. All the booths are taken.

Oberbaumbrücke, upper-tree-bridge, marks one of the borders between the old East and West. The trees – medieval barriers that blocked the passage of ships – pen in the river: it flows into the city at the Oberbaum and leaves the city at the Unterbaum. Underneath the bridge, two neon hands face each other from either side of the black water, from either side of history. They change position and colour every six seconds. When you show the hands to others, you are surprised by how long it takes them to figure out the pattern.[2] You want the hands to make all your decisions for you.

A talking jackal with glowing eyes stops you at the S-Bahn station to tell you: A heart brought you here, but it will take another organ to get you out. If you can harness its power.[3] The environment is only rendered where you are standing. Beyond that, the pixels haven't had a chance to wake up, dress themselves, brush their teeth.

---

2 <*Stein-Papier-Schere* (1997) art installation by Thorsten Goldberg.>
3 <This scene is from *I Have No Mouth, And I Must Scream.* Peak 1990s puzzle game frustration. And on top of that, famous dickhead Harlan Ellison intentionally made it impossible to win. A walkthrough is a must.>

A BAD CASE

Darragh McCausland

It used to be so different. In brighter days, long gone, before I ever picked up a drink, there seemed endless worlds but only ever one beginning: a torch-lit stone corridor or room viewed from a fixed point. Inside it were the necessary rudiments of adventure, drawn with the poetical economy of pixel art. Small details, such as a skull or a single broken spear, indicated the peril ahead. Somewhere behind, above, or around that space, there was me in my Green Day T-shirt, peering through the oily curtains of my hair, the ruthless thirteen-year-old commander of a party of four familiar figures: warrior, priest, archer and mage. Safety and comfort reside there, in that simulation of peril. A tantalizing shred of that feeling, once so vast it was as if the whole universe were an endless duvet made from bedroom air, can come back to me whenever I see a screenshot or clip of a favoured game from the time. Just enough to know that there was a place that once existed where the imagination could roam through endless gentle fields of thought. Just enough, too, to feel the anguish of the irretrievable loss of that Elysian place.

That was how it was. The comforts of role-playing games turned out to be transitory, perhaps due to permanent changes in a limbic system that had to manage a near permanent feeling of 'being hunted'. The great original feeling diminished rapidly and could only be experienced through painfully incomplete sensory echoes like a drug that can no longer get you high. I searched for it elsewhere and found it, in the usual dangerous places. At the age of fourteen alcohol became my comforter and it flowed through the subsequent two and half decades of my life as an increasingly opaque and torrential river that smashes everything to shit, takes everything with it. The afternoon I eventually returned to seek comfort in a role-playing game, which came a couple of days after the wheels spun off what might be called my 'entire life', the game had necessarily changed.

In this desperate place there is no party of four. It shrinks down to one playable character, a broken middle-aged policeman named Harry who lies face down in his Y-fronts in an overwhelmingly brown and dingy isometric space. It's not technically a dungeon, though you might call it a dungeon. In place of spears, skulls and torches, there are broken bottles, discarded clothes, wallpaper that has the exact pattern of the carpet from the Overlook Hotel in *The Shining*, a soiled mattress and a rotating ceiling fan from which a necktie dangles ominously, horribly. An omniscient voiceover that knows more than Harry (who, like me, is coming around from the worst bender of his life and knows fuck all other than things are very bad indeed, cosmically bad) intones, 'all recollections of the person you are, the people in your life and the world you're in have drowned in a sea of blood alcohol'. Oh shit, I think, and I'm instantly hooked.

With a trembling grip, barely quieted by the 350 mg of Lyrica I've abused in a wild DIY attempt to blunt alcohol withdrawal, I take my computer mouse in hand. I manipulate Harry's sprite around his thrashed surrounds. I figure out, as he interacts with items, that he is in a hostel room above a dive bar and that the person who thrashed it was him. After a few moments of such interactions, I steer him towards his initial encounter, which in any other game would be with a recognizable stock foe, some low-level kobold or goblin type creature. But *Disco Elysium* is not any other game and the 'enemy' that Harry faces, in what will turn out to be perhaps the most significant encounter in his story, is his own reflection in a filthy bathroom mirror. Or, to be precise, is not the reflection itself, but the vicious thought process that occurs in him when he sees it. How he fares on seeing it is determined, in the manner of *Dungeons & Dragons*, by two dice rolls. The first, to establish whether Harry can even recognize the grotesque grinning vision that meets his gaze as his own face. The second dice roll is a trickier prospect. It is to ascertain how he handles 'the Expression', which, according to the game's text, is his alcoholic defence against reality, a rictus clownish smirk that seems permanently frozen on his unhealthy face. It's a brutal thing to look at, a 'death mask' that hides an inner despair with no bottom.

Thanks to the game's expressionistic art style, it is presented in all its vast horror. Like a painterly image from a graphic novel, it expands slowly and dreadfully, filling the entire screen with Harry's unkempt has-been hair and beard, his red-nosed, sweaty and desperately beseeching grimace. Light flashes. His sprite clutches its grey chest as if lanced by a sword. He has failed the dice roll. In the lower left corner of the display, his morale drops by one. My own morale, which at that instant becomes utterly wedded to his, in an intense symbiotic relationship that will last for the four full days I'll play the game at the start of the most harrowing twelve months of my life, inches momentarily up. Why? Because in this washed-up character, who is by turns deluded, grandiose, selfish, sentimental and grovelling, and whose deepest animating feelings relate to abandonment, rejection and loss, I have found the perfect avatar of myself and the appalling circumstances into which my addiction has delivered me. Lieutenant Harry Du Bois, the amnesiac, disco-loving detective brought in to investigate a suspicious death in the Martinaise district of the ruined and melancholy city of Revanchol, is no ordinary alcoholic. He is on a whole other level. He is what my father would call, with a look of knowing finality in his upset eyes, 'a bad case'.

My father has always had the ability to charge otherwise innocuous words with bleak forces. The power comes from his face when he says them. Once the words become imbued with it, the effect is irreversible, and the result is that little turns of phrase said to me at moments of extreme confrontational pressure exist permanently among the rooms of my inner life like inscriptions above doors. Like one Tuesday afternoon in the kitchen of our family home, when I sat at the table trying to hold eye contact with him as my head lurched forward. That morning, my intoxication had been a mystery because every drop of ethanol had not only been removed from the house, but the front and back doors had been locked. My father, however, was a diligent detective in matters concerning my degeneracy. He had discovered a perfect Adidas Hamburg-shaped footprint on the inside sill of the downstairs bedroom where I slept. With a speck of foam on his mouth, he held my wrist and said, 'There's fuckin plenty of people who can't drink but you're worse than that. You're a bad case.' No stupor could have withstood the power of his facial expression. I'd call it lost hope, but those words can't hold it. The effect was imparted in its totality in what a sensitive art critic standing in front of a Rothko might classify as 'perfect transference'. This was a year before I encountered Harry Du Bois. I was living at home for a summer to give my wife a reprieve from my addiction, a dress rehearsal for the terminal events of the following year, when the entire world would hibernate on account of a virus and my drinking would reach levels of self-destruction that I still struggle to comprehend.

The total received effect of an artwork depends not only on the artist's initial effort, but on the beholder's capacity to meet it halfway and imagine themselves into it. There is work involved on both sides. In his Büchner Prize-winning speech from 1960, the poet Paul Celan names the mysterious field where this interaction takes place as 'The Meridian'. In days of good health, I had not only a robust and healthy capacity but a hungry urge to meet all variety of vision and experience in art. I wanted to swim past the substance of myself and reach 'the other' in fabulous outward-looking places of the mind. Life's rich pageantry marched through the portals of all the paintings, poems and books I consumed. Then alcoholism, a disease of solipsism, took me into its vice. When it became active in me over sustained periods, booze became the fuel that powered a steam train of self-obsession. The entire universe had to narrow down to fit through the bottleneck of self. Any desire to encounter 'the other' was obliterated. It was like the scene in Charlie Kaufman's *Being John Malkovich* where John Malkovich enters a portal into his own subconscious and finds himself in a malignant dimension where the face of every human being and animal is now his face, and the language they speak is composed of one repeating word: Malkovich. During ferocious, constrictive periods of drunkenness that lasted over months, my interests in art narrowed accordingly. All I wanted to see or feel was a version of me, reflected at me. In pungent, close environments with pulled curtains and my bottle of Huzzar never far from hand, I'd obsessively watch or read anything I could find about alcoholics of the worst stripe. Terminal fuck-ups. Unfixable end-stage cases. People beyond all hope. Stuff like *Leaving Las Vegas* or Jack Kerouac's *Big Sur.*

Can I say it did me any good? It did something for me. There was certainly comfort in it, but it would be a stretch to call it therapeutic. My mind could appreciate those characters and their awful travails, and it fed off them in some vampiric way, but it was too broken to inhabit them meaningfully. I perceived them vaguely, passingly and at a remove, as if they were floating things behind aquarium glass. They wouldn't have saved me the time it really mattered. That was the day my brother, who was almost as diligent a detective of my degeneracy as my father, discovered me passed out in a bed decorated with dried vomit in my soon-to-be-not-my apartment, three days after my wife made the long-fated but still somehow startling decision to leave me for good. Close by me, my brother found an item I had bought with the ornate and futile hopes of any addict who attempts an alternative hobby to poisoning themself, a bread lame for slashing the living skin of sourdough bread. I had placed it there manipulatively, to suggest a suicide attempt. With hard and bitter words, my brother pulled me from that room where four days' worth of discarded bottles glinted horribly in stale half-light. I was eventually deposited onto the 109 bus that ran the main route of my life, from Dublin to the family home in Kells. I made a human scarecrow on it. I remember pressing my moist forehead against the window glass and watching yellow fields of rapeseed scroll past as I talked to myself in a low, shell-shocked patter. That time when it really mattered, I needed a different type of a character in a different type of medium. I needed Harry.

The day after my brother found me, once I had deleted all my social media and Messenger apps in a reality-denying frenzy, I purchased *Disco Elysium* and downloaded it onto my computer. The numbing medicine of alcohol was suddenly gone and anxiety closed around me from every angle, squeezing terrors from me like old air pouring through the neck of a balloon. Only a big container could begin to receive all that pain, some vast distraction. A role-playing game might do it. I knew very little about the game I chose, only that it had an isometric viewpoint (my favourite nostalgic style, where the structures are like three-dimensional dollhouses), that it was described as 'a detective role-playing game,' and, most importantly, that it took on average forty hours to complete.

The purchase occurred not long before 8.27 pm on Tuesday, 2 June 2020. I can say this with confidence. In researching this essay I redownloaded the game from the cloud to refresh my knowledge of it and I found all my original save games were exactly where I left them. They made a descending set of rectangles with precise time stamps that ran for four days during the Covid heatwave. The cloud had kept a record. A filing cabinet of pain.

Those files, which run from the evening of 2 June to 11.32 am on 6 June (the point I completed the game and got a 'bad ending' because I made deliberately toxic choices while playing Harry) put pause to my plans for the essay. If I'm honest, they derailed me. There was this staggering burst of memory-feeling brought on by the mere sight of them. It was potent, unexpected and not without alarm bells, real danger. It was analogous to Proust's famous madeleine, except in place of the sensual ecstasy his narrator experienced as the full past opened around him like a lotus flower, I sensed an excruciating and dreadful slime of impression that had me shrink from the screen. A sudden spectral overlay obscured the present. My old childhood bedroom. The place I always ended up when all else collapsed. Drawn curtains, with fabric patterned like the inside of a savoy cabbage, glowed green against the sunlight that raked the world I cringed and hid from. From a room below, a sound rose in a blare softened by carpet. The ominous dipping and surging theme of ITV's daytime game show *Tipping Point*. My father, the only person in the world who knew where my shoes and wallet were, watched its tumbling discs with one eye. His other eye was trained on the glass panels of the door I'd have to pass should I try to escape the house. A smell enveloped me, my bedsheets and all my clothes. Evidence of poisoning perhaps? It was like fermenting banana.

Now here's a suspicious thought. If I could experience all that from merely looking at the save game files, what might happen if I clicked through on one of them? Would I get the full IMAX experience of repressed and incomprehensible terrors, locked away since that summer because a mind that must protect its own sanity can only withstand a fixed amount of pain? I thought of the ghost containment unit in *Ghostbusters* and the very powerful ideas it stirred in me when I watched that film at a young age. I knew that there was more to it than what the surface told us. I knew that even though it was only the size of a walk-in fridge, it contained enough ghosts to haunt the biggest city in America. A ghost containment unit is a terrible thing.

My initial vision for this essay was for it to be a wide-ranging, detailed and even luxurious critical analysis of *Disco Elysium* as a stunning artistic portrayal of an alcoholic. It'd spare no effort in exploring the game's many systems, its dialogue and its flavourful art style to draw out what it is that makes it so special. It'd pay particular attention to the atmosphere of Harry's world, Revachol, and how the aching musical soundtrack composed by the band Sea Power breathes through it. It'd mention, for sure, the Whirling-In-Rags motif, where a guitar melody, augmented by a frost-touched trumpet from a faraway place, sounds like ennui itself. That was the plan, until those save files fucked it.

But no matter, because others have gone before me. Any rudimentary search of YouTube will throw up no end of material on *Disco Elysium*'s artistic merits. There's an abundance of video essays that follow a similar format. Four-hour jobs that take four hundred hours to make, presented by dictionary-licking men who know their way around a little predigested French theory and a lot of Reddit. It's all there waiting for a deep dive. Their discourse is not without its merits.

I can't abandon the vision completely, however. I at least owe the kernel of what was to be my argument. It can, fortuitously enough, be summed up in a single word. Complicity. That word can be illustrated in a moment I remember experiencing early in the game. In the Whirling-In-Rags bar, a little darkened patch of countertop became highlighted when I clicked on it, inviting an interaction from Harry. It turned out to be spilled rum. A box dialogue opened on screen, describing Harry's thinking and the actions he might choose to do. One of these was the option to try to lick the spilled rum off the counter. Only a few days prior to encountering this moment in the game, I had found myself shivering and desperate and weaving a lonely lap of Dublin's Smithfield square in that dreadful and endless hour before the off-licence opened. The Covid pandemic was at its early height and the square's seagull-monitored desertion lent everything a faintly post-apocalyptic tinge. Something winked at me from the top of a wheelie bin. A red wine bottle. It had a shadowy dreg inside it. Without any hesitation, I drank it. So, of course, I also got Harry to try to lick the counter. And therein lies the connection I forged with that character. When watching a film – say Nicolas Cage's character Ben in *Leaving Las Vegas* – I am an observer. Whereas with Harry, I became his co-conspirator. At every possible turn in that play-through I made him do any shitty shameful thing I was allowed. My recovering friend Josh talks often and joyfully about how the universe conspires in his favour, usually by putting people in his path when he needs them most. Even though Harry is just a character in a game, I believe that is how it worked out between the two of us. I was able to become him and make him lick rum off a counter. And it helped me.

There is a line of dialogue that sticks with me. It comes when Harry takes his first drink in the game, from a voice in his Thought Cabinet, which is made up of the psychological traits that modify his abilities in the game.

'You've been here before,' it says. 'Welcome back, detective. You're home now.'

I used to feel safe at home in games, but now I find safety resides in good habits. Most evenings, our family convenes as a party of four on the L-shaped IKEA couch. Dinner is eaten at the kitchen table, but dessert is here, taken in front of a downloaded episode of the early 2000s science fiction series *Lost*. We've evolved eccentrically in what we eat, no longer ice pops, but rhubarb yoghurts from Lidl, frozen hard and attacked with teaspoons. Iris, the eleven-year-old, is usually on yoghurt duty. One night, not so long ago, when she left the room to go outside to fetch yoghurts from the freezer in the shed, I followed her in my mind, which roams a little freer than it did when I met Harry. I pictured her walking through the garden where the walls stand close and narcissi nod in the dark. My laptop was open on my lap, on the *Disco Elysium* save screen. My mind switched from Iris to a madly specific memory of me trudging around on my own in a field behind Kells swimming pool one murky autumn afternoon after school. I was around Iris's age. I had a mandarin in my bag that I didn't want to eat. I held it and looked at it and said out loud, as exhilaration rose through me, 'nobody alive ever gets to see what the inside of this mandarin looks like,' then I flung it into a deep and stagnant drain.

I do not open the files. I delete them one by one.

A HELL TAXONOMY (ON DOOM, 1993)

Roisin Kiberd

Hell hath no limits, nor is circumscrib'd
In one self place; for where we are is hell,
And where hell is, there must we ever be.
– Christopher Marlowe, *Doctor Faustus*

1. Irish Hell

Hell is in the midlands: Rathcroghan, the largest unexcavated royal site in Europe, a network of burial mounds and ringforts built over 5,500 years. It was once home to Medb, the warrior queen. It is also a door to the underworld.

Hell is in the north, at St Patrick's Purgatory, another ancient site, this time in Donegal. Where Rathcroghan is the domain of pagan gods, this is its Christian counterpart: a cave revealed to Patrick by Christ himself, offering a glimpse of the inferno. Patrick used it as an educational tool, for scaring the locals into converting.

Hell lives in Galway, or rather, a celebrated architect of hell. Romero Games, the video game company founded in 2015 by Brenda and John Romero, has its offices just off Eyre Square. John Romero has worked on over 130 games, founded eight companies and won over 100 awards for his work as a game designer and programmer. He made his name in the early 1990s as a founding member of id Software, the developers who gave the world the first-person shooter, the deathmatch and the goriest, grisliest, most hellish games the world had ever seen.

At midnight on 10 December 1993, after roughly one year of working with all the febrile enthusiasm of twenty-somethings fed on heavy metal, horror films and pizza, id Software released *Doom*, its genre-defining first-person shooter. You play as the 'space marine' Doomguy, a tough, nameless motherfucker with a shotgun and a pixelated brush cut. Sent to Mars as punishment for insubordination, he faces down legions of demons before it's revealed that, through experimentation with teleports, scientists have accidentally opened a portal to hell, and the demons have overrun Earth.

Doom raised the bar, not only for gameplay, but for gore. Rich in blood, guts and satanic imagery, it birthed a new kind of moral panic; critics labelled it a 'mass murder simulator'. Both of the Columbine shooters were *Doom* fans (in a video made on the day of his killing spree, Eric Harris even claimed 'It's going to be like fucking *Doom*'). Media outlets treated the game as dangerous – one paper claimed it could 'widen the hole in any kid's soul' – while then-President Bill Clinton used his weekly radio address to highlight *Doom*'s role in 'a culture that too often glorifies violence.' In 2001, id Software was named in a lawsuit filed by families of Columbine victims, along with entertainment companies including Nintendo, Sega and Time Warner Inc. The case was eventually dismissed.

I'm fascinated by moral panics relating to media and art; they attribute a near-mystical power to their target, whether it's a book, a film, music (played backwards, preferably) or a video game. The larger the panic, the stronger this power becomes. Ultimately, moral panics highlight the transformative potential in art, one which we often overlook until it's seen to go wrong.

Doom was transformative in so many ways; it introduced a new form of gaming, unprecedented in its violence and its possibilities for customization. Perhaps this is why religious organizations and politicians wished to censor it. 'They did criticize it,' said John Romero, speaking to me over Skype from the Galway offices of Romero Games, 'but we never paid attention to that, because, you know, everybody loved it.'

This is no exaggeration. *Doom* was a phenomenon, a moment in tech and gaming history on par with the launch of the iPhone, or Windows 95, but a lot more metal. The night *Doom* launched shops were mobbed, whole university computer networks broke down and systems belonging to schools, corporations and even government facilities ground to a halt due to the number of people trying to play it. 'It was the most fun thing anyone had played,' said Romero. 'People were going out and buying computers just to play the game, and networking got massive, because the game supported it.'

Doom established a genre, a way of playing and an aesthetic that endure to this day. New first-person shooters are released every year, their protagonists walking in the frenzied footsteps of Doomguy. There have been eight *Doom* sequels and four *Doom* spin-offs, and fans continue to convene for Deathmatch tournaments, where players battle each other in a bloody free-for-all.

Decades have passed, but *Doom* still feels current. It continues to attract players across generations, not only for its gameplay or its place in history, but because it taps into something eternal: our fear of – and fascination with – hell.

2. A Map of Hell

There is a hell for almost every culture. Aztec hell contains jaguars and rivers of blood. Zoroastrianism details a 'House of Lies', while Jain cosmology features a hell built on seven levels – you won't have to stay there forever, but it may take several billion years to get out. In ancient Mesopotamia hell was dry and dusty, and the living poured libations on the ground for departed relatives to drink. In the Apocalypse of Paul, hell has rivers of fire, but also rivers of ice for the cold-hearted. Dante's hell is highly structured and delivered in cantos, with levels for those who indulged wrath, lust, greed and so on. The Christian hell is rich in imagery and specific detail; it's a hell made for artists, writers and designers of video games.

In 2018, Pope Francis is said to have denied the existence of hell in an interview with Eugenio Scalfari, a journalist he had spoken with on several occasions. In response, the Vatican stated that Scalfari's article was not 'a faithful transcription of the words of the Holy Father' – a convenient claim, given that the interview was apparently held in private, and not recorded.

Even if hell has been cancelled, we will continue to visit it in video games, where each day new conscripts are lured to the inferno. On Steam, the online video game marketplace, a search for the term 'hell' gives 22,781 results, suggesting games like *Hell Blade*, *Hellbound* and *Waifu Hell*, a hentai game where you alternate between ogling and shooting at naked, levitating women.

Shortly before *Doom* was created, in late 1992, the id team was heavily involved in a *Dungeons & Dragons* campaign, with co-founder John Carmack acting as Dungeon Master. Romero tried to procure a magic sword and caused the earth to be overrun by demons, inspiring, quite suddenly, the premise for Carmack and Romero's next game. It's worth adding here that *Dungeons & Dragons* was itself the subject of a moral panic; in the early 1980s TSR, Inc., the company that produced it, was sued by anti-occult group BADD, which stands for 'Bothered About Dungeons and Dragons'. BADD linked the game to 'blasphemy, suicide, assassination, insanity, sex perversion, homosexuality, prostitution, satanic-type rituals, gambling, barbarism, cannibalism' and other practices. The lawsuit was dismissed.

The id team worked with a copy of H.R. Giger's *Necronomicon* on the table in front of them, and the name, famously, came from a Tom Cruise line in *The Color of Money* ('What's in the case?' 'In here? Doom.'). 'When we made it, back then, we just started with a bunch of gruesome images,' said Romero. 'Blood lakes, twisted faces, all kinds of stuff we found unnerving. And then just a lot of burning stuff. Pentagrams, you know?'

The aesthetic influence of horror films – as well as their ghoulish humour and their spirit of low-budget audacity – is palpable in *Doom*, as in id Software's earlier classic, *Wolfenstein 3D*, and, later, the wildly successful *Quake*. 'Basically it was *Evil Dead*, and *Aliens*, and *Dungeons & Dragons* and heavy metal,' said Romero. 'It was all those things mixed together, with dark humour and a shotgun and chainsaws. We wanted it to be like in *Aliens*, with lots of stuff coming at you. Hordes of bad things! And that fear that you felt with *Alien*, because it's dark, and you don't know what's around the corner, but you hear the noises…'

Doom was built to showcase technologies that had never been used in games before. As designer, Romero played through each level repeatedly, refining it, until he had run through each one hundreds, even thousands of times. Carmack built an improved graphics engine, with binary space partitioning and texture-mapping; shadows deepened at a distance, ceilings slanted menacingly, and walls contained secrets and interactive panels. The design was murky, mutable and brilliantly sinister, lending a chiaroscuro horror to proceedings even before the monsters arrived.

Doom's other surprise was its subject matter, which turned out to be rooted in religious imagery as much as in science fiction. Romero said, 'The thing about *Doom* was that instead of humans meeting aliens in space, which is what you'd expect, you're meeting *hell* instead… It's as if hell really exists, and now it's something you actually have to deal with.' Romero cited H.P. Lovecraft as an influence – in fact the final boss of *Doom*'s follow-up, *Quake*, is the Hell-Mother, a direct import from Lovecraft's Cthulhu Mythos. 'It was always a question of doing something different, and interesting, that we hadn't seen before. *Quake* had a Lovecraft influence in terms of the feel of the game – that constant, unsettling feeling that something is wrong. It was hyper-violent, and anything could happen, so you had to stay on your toes.'

3. Hell as Bestiary

I'll tell you about the imaginary beings you meet in hell. They move in ways unfamiliar to humans: scuttling, sailing through air, issuing squelching, moaning sounds that haunt you long after you take off your headphones. The creatures of *Doom* strain at the limits of 1990s technology. They possess a physicality I find deeply unnerving.

The Imp, *Doom*'s most mundane enemy, is sludge-coloured and easily defeated. Its eyes blaze red, while its face is fixed in a strained rictus of shock.

The Mancubus is a mass of seething flesh, a slightly more mobile cousin to Jabba the Hutt. It has two flame-throwers for hands, and its death is spectacular; an implosion of blood and viscera, body collapsing, head exploding, green glowing eyeballs that fall to the floor.

The Cacodemon is *Doom*'s mascot: one-eyed, blazing red like an inflamed organ. It pulsates smugly in the air, spitting out flame balls. Its death is a lesson in occult anatomy; it spurts red blood when you shoot it, but bleeds blue goop when it finally dies.

The Pain Elemental, found in *Doom II*, the best-named creature has a single red eye, horns, an otherworldly croak, and futile little T. rex arms. Kill a Pain Elemental and it splits itself into three Lost Souls, floating skulls that blaze across the room.

The Spider Mastermind, leader of *Doom*'s battalion, is a kind of Krang 2.0 crossed with the robot from *Wild Wild West*. When you finally defeat it, its metal body breaks apart and only its leering teeth remain.

Musclebound, red, with the legs of a goat, the Baron of Hell emits a cosmic darkness. Sometimes I worry that if I look at one too long, I will become sexually attracted to it. The Hell Knight is a weaker, smaller relative of the Baron of Hell, while the Cyberdemon is its gigantic, Minotaur-like godfather.

The Arch Vile, lurching and spindly, is perhaps *Doom*'s eeriest creation due to how closely he resembles a human. Tall and bald and emaciated, his ribcage protrudes across his contorted back. Sometimes he throws up his arms, as if giving thanks for the chance to kill you.

Finally there's the Icon of Sin, the boss of bosses, a wall-mounted goat head. Projectiles emerge from its wound, a flash of rosy exposed brain. Its eyes are dead, its mouth smiling. It is sometimes referred to as 'Baphomet'. Approach the Icon of Sin, leap into its wound, and you'll find the game's true nemesis: an Easter egg, the ultimate Oz-behind-the-curtain moment in gaming. You'll see a familiar head impaled on a stick, speaking backwards in the game designer's own voice: 'To win the game, you must kill me, John Romero.'

You shoot him, but hasn't he already won?

4. Hell as Other Players

Inspired by games like *Street Fighter II*, which the team played during breaks, Romero proposed the Deathmatch during *Doom*'s development. Up to four players could battle over a local network, or two could use a modem. 'This is the first game to really exploit the power of LANs and modems to their full potential,' id wrote in a *Doom* press release. 'In 1993, we fully expect to be the number one cause of decreased productivity in businesses around the world.'

Doom is also credited with popularizing the mod, or 'modification', a customized version of a game created by its fans. Mods can add new levels, objects, weapons, settings or characters. Modding was – and remains today – a popular first step for future game designers.

During our conversation, Romero noted the difficulties that prevent modding communities from forming around games today. 'Now when you talk about any big game it's basically un-moddable,' he said, 'because the games are so complex.' The exception is if a company specifically wants to encourage mods: 'You have to deliberately open it up and let people in, and make specific tools to help them mod.'

Doom arrived at precisely the right time in history, a point when the hacker ethic crossed over into popular culture. The game was customizable from its inception. Soon there was *Doom Simpsons*, *Doom* in a shopping mall, and even *Marine Doom*, created by and for the US Marine Corps as a training aid. Today, versions of *Doom* number in the tens of thousands. Recently there was *BorderDoom*, a mashup with *Borderlands*, the gory *Meatgrinder Co-op* and *Brutal Minecraft*, which is as it sounds, a shoot-em-up set in the wholesome, pixel-bricked world of *Minecraft*.

In this sense, *Doom* keeps alive the DIY ethic of early gaming, an industry largely created by teenagers making games at home, the way Soundcloud rappers build careers from their laptops today. 'The entire industry was founded on indies,' Romero said, 'and it still *is* indies that are pushing the boundaries with new ideas.' Romero himself began by making such games; as a teenager in the 1980s he sent homemade games to magazines, where they were printed as code (readers would type the entire programme into their computers in order to play them).

As well as mods and Deathmatches, id Software gave the world another small yet crucial trope in modern gaming: the presence of a hand – the protagonist's hand, more often than not holding a weapon, and always positioned at the bottom of the screen. This hand first appeared not in *Doom*, or even in *Wolfenstein 3D*, but in its precursor, id's 1991 title *Catacomb 3D*, where you play as a high wizard battling skeletons and reapers with spells that shoot from your fingertips.

The hand came back for *Wolfenstein*, then for *Doom* and later for *Quake*, by which time it had become an industry norm. There's something richly symbolic about this hand. Instead of a figure like Virgil to guide you through the underworld, it invites you to guide yourself. Here are limitless levels of hell that you can build yourself – a customized hell, different for every player. Much like the plot of *Doom*, its creators opened a portal that seems likely never to close.

When I asked Romero how it feels to have created something potentially eternal, he compared it to something unexpected: exotica music, the genre created by composer Martin Denny in 1950s America. 'Martin Denny started to create this Hawaiian jazz-lounge music, but he added animal and bird noises to it,' said Romero. 'He created a whole band where people were making animal noises – because who can teach frogs to make sounds on command? The people who were in his band after they finished repeated that idea, and continued to make exotica in their own style.' Exotica's afterlife was earned through its inherent strangeness: 'It died out after some point, but it lasted for decades. That was very niche back then, whereas *Doom* is huge in gaming, and is still going strong twenty-six years later. With the new games coming out too, *Doom* will definitely see a fiftieth anniversary.'

5. Production Hell

Often I suspect that the gruelling quality of certain games hints at the circumstances in which they were made. From documentaries, and from watching game designers have occasional Twitter breakdowns, I get a sense of the industry as vampiric, attracting talented young outcasts and draining them of life. Much like writers, game designers suffer for their art in deeply unglamorous ways: mood swings, instability, caffeine dependence and fighting with co-workers (if you have them – another thing I notice is how lonely the process of making a game can be). Designers' work requires persistence in the face of hopelessness – in the face of releasing a title that might never be reviewed, and will sell on Steam for a median price of $5.99.

John Romero knows about production hell. Work was delayed for years on his game *Daikatana*, a first-person shooter set in futuristic Japan, Ancient Greece, Norway in the Dark Ages and finally, a futuristic San Francisco. Ideas clashed, one game engine was swapped for another and the company's office, an extravagant penthouse, caused problems when it turned out that light from the ceiling prevented employees from seeing their screens. After multiple missed launch dates, staff departures, an overrun budget and an infamous print ad that declared that 'John Romero's about to make you his bitch', *Daikatana* was released to poor reviews and angry players in the year 2000.

Even in the earlier days at id Software's office, 'Suite 666', the team seems to have worked in permanent crunch mode. David Kushner's book *Masters of Doom* reveals that their office was next to a dentist's; the sound of drills and, occasionally, screams drifted in through the wall, inspiring the demonic ambience of *Doom*. *Wolfenstein 3D* was made in roughly seven months, while *Doom* took just over a year. *Doom II* was released the following year, and two years after that id Software put out *Quake*. Each of these games were hugely successful and influential, and their teams faced conflict, tight deadlines, no sleep and a diet of pizza in order to pull this off.

'You put into the game what you're feeling,' said Romero. 'It's something I think a lot of people don't pay attention to. With *Quake*, the mood was that everyone was expecting to have put a game out already, but we weren't able to because the technology wasn't ready. People were creating things they'd then have to delete, or make massive changes to, because the engine wasn't finished. We didn't know it was going to take that long.' If the designer's mood can influence a game, then perhaps a game can influence its creators in turn. *Quake*, with its brutal gameplay and nightmarish tone, was the product of an arduous creative process: 'That disturbing, unsettling feeling in the game needed to happen, no matter how we were feeling. So that's what we made.'

Within the last three decades, the game industry has grown to a market value of roughly $148 billion, and game development has changed accordingly. '*Assassin's Creed*, as one example, could have over a thousand people working on the game,' Romero said. 'It's massive. It's hard to have a really strong creative force driven into a game, to the heart of it, to make sure it stays true to its vision.'

It strikes me that the industry runs on extremes of over- and under-staffing, with larger titles sometimes bloated and over-financed, while indie games rely on one or two fanatically devoted creators to see them into the world. Perhaps this is why so many of the indie games that stand out to me are framed as a journey through the protagonist's fraying mind – titles like *The Beginner's Guide*, or *Braid* or *Amnesia: The Dark Descent*, or even *Hotline Miami*, with its claustrophobic sleaze and hallucinatory violence.

I am, evidently, not the first person to romanticize the highs and lows of creative employment; as I write this, a TV show is in the works about the early days of id Software, based on *Masters of Doom*. I know it's wrong to valorize exhaustion, not least in the context of larger development companies, but there's something I admire deeply about people who make video games: a kind of madness, an alienation and desire to be heard, which I see in writers too. It's a job that's contradictory to its core, requiring independence of thought, coupled with an almost maniacal need to reach people. It requires control, purpose, dedication and, finally, the ability to give your project away and see it reinterpreted by everyone else.

6. Screen Hell

In recent years I've played several games set in the underworld. There's *Undertale*, which I never finished, a kind of anti-*Pokémon* where you're given the chance either to talk to monsters or fight them. *Pinstripe*, an indie game about a self-destructive former minister, is set in a hell that's snowbound and lonely, while in *Limbo*, by far my favourite, you play as a boy running through a forest in black and white, searching for his lost sister.

These are not violent games; they're more like meditations, dismantling the tropes of gaming to ask questions about agency and guilt. They treat the screen as a canvas for spiritual inquiry. They ask what it is about hell that keeps us coming back.

I started working on this essay in Berlin at the end of the summer 2020, shortly before moving back to Dublin. I began with the very enjoyable research task of playing *Wolfenstein 3D*. What made the game more fun was my understanding that it was banned in the country where I was playing it; due to section 86a of Germany's criminal code, which forbids depictions of symbols linked with unconstitutional organizations (even if the point of the game is to mow down Nazis), *Wolfenstein* and its sequels were illegal. I was wrong: a 2018 court ruling granted 'case-by-case examinations' of controversial material, and *Wolfenstein 3D* was made legal. It's still great, for the record, but it was more fun when I thought it was banned.

I grew up in an Ireland slowly making peace with its urge to censor, allowing the public to draw its own conclusions on morality and art. In the 1990s and early 2000s almost all the banned books were allowed, but video shops had entire shelves of yellow-stickered 'extreme' films like *Baise-moi* or *A Clockwork Orange*, made all the more enticing by their warnings, which implied that you *could* watch them, but at a risk to your own integrity, and possibly your soul. Video games took this sense of agency and possibility even further, landing the player in the middle of the action and inviting them to kill or be killed, to resist or embrace their own damnation.

Another game I enjoy, *Hotline Miami*, famously asks 'Do you like hurting other people?' I don't. In fact, I spend a ridiculous amount of time, in everyday life, worrying about hurting people by accident. Yet I love first-person shooters, top-down shooters, games where I shoot zombies or mutants or fascists or pixelated monsters. I rely on them in times of stress, playing with such fanatical consistency that my coffee goes cold and I lose sleep and little animated guns flash behind my eyelids for hours after I stop playing. My Steam account is a home for my contradictions as a person, a place to indulge murderous impulses I lack outside the screen.

I suspect the majority of games hold a latent morality, a prospect *Doom* interrogates with grisly irreverence. Why does it pit technology against the demons of hell, as though they're forces as strong as each other? The default skill level in *Doom* is called 'Hurt Me Plenty'. Do I enjoy hurting other people? Do I enjoy hurting myself?

Or have I absorbed by osmosis a view from American headlines printed when I was a child: the belief that a game might be too dangerous to play, and can damage the soul of its player?

7. Hell International

In Tartarus you don't die, because you're already dead. Instead you simply fail, again and again, at repetitive tasks, exhausting, futile, almost murderous in their mundanity. These are dark nursery rhymes, morality tales that lack an ending.

King Ixion is tied to a flaming wheel for lechery and the murder of his father-in-law. Sisyphus is made to push a boulder up a hill, only for it to fall down again. The Danaïdes, husband-murderers of legend, are forced to carry water in a jug to a bath, but the jug is full of holes. King Tantalus, after murdering his son, is condemned to stand in water, starving and parched, under a branch bearing perfectly ripe fruit. Each time he reaches for fruit, the tree pulls it away, and when he stoops to drink the water it drains away too.

In Ireland, before de Valera, before Archbishop John Charles McQuaid, before the British and before even Catholicism itself, our own pagan 'hell' was a place notable for its moral ambivalence. We didn't really have hell, just an all-purpose Otherworld, built without segregation.

In Celtic mythology, the Otherworld is not a place of punishment but a land of happiness. It's elusive – 'other', but never very far away. It's known by multiple names, in multiple permutations – Tír na nÓg, Mag Mell, Mag Cíuin and Hy-Brasil, the phantom island located in the mists to the west. In some myths it's even called Tír na mBeo, the 'Land of the Living'; its residents are not dead, but alive forever. The Celts ran into battle fearless, because they believed they would endure beyond death. Their Otherworld could even be accessed from our one; burial mounds, and openings such as the Cave of the Cats (Oweynagat) at Rathcroghan, allowed passage between the two worlds, at Samhain and at Bealtaine.

As a Catholic, however lapsed, I find it a challenge to imagine an afterlife without the prospect of damnation. It feels central to morality, and to our national identity, however far we progress from our roots. It's woven into our language; after St Patrick arrived we learned to threaten each other with curses. One goes '*Go n-ithe an cat thú is go n-ithe an diabhal an cat*' ('May a cat eat you, and may the devil eat the cat'). Another is '*Go ndéana an diabhal dréimire de cnámh do dhroma ag piocadh úll i ngairdín Ifrinn*' ('May the devil make a ladder of your backbone, so that he can pick apples in the garden of hell'). Finally, in the late twentieth century, the earnest discussion of hell became unfashionable, and we consigned it to video games.

Rathcroghan, the hell-gate in Roscommon, is a site older than the Egyptian pyramids. At face value the Cave of the Cats is an unprepossessing hole in the ground, but it's also a place of pilgrimage. On YouTube there are videos shot by tourists; the person holding the camera climbs down, through darkness, into an oblivion of stones. Each video ends with a return to the light; they always stop before they reach the Otherworld.

In legend the cave functions like a teleport; a cow is dragged in and emerges a short time later, one county over, from the Caves of Kesh. Then there are the monsters that emerge; the Ellén Trechend, three-headed and scaly; the werewolves; the swarms of red birds and feral swine that wither crops with their breath before vanishing. There are the giant wildcats, which give the cave its name, and the Morrigan, goddess of war and fate, who sometimes takes the form of a crow. In legend the Morrigan emerges from the cave in a chariot pulled by a one-legged horse, a detail that strikes me as extremely metal.

I imagine the Celts and their baffled Christian successors repeating stories about a cave in the midlands simply to amuse themselves, and not guessing these stories would endure for over a thousand years. The cow-teleportation and the three-headed beasts remind me of games we play today; they prove that we keep the bad things close – but not *too* close – because it makes life more exciting.

8. 'In Hell is All Manner of Delight'

The above line is spoken by Lucifer in *Doctor Faustus*, Christopher Marlowe's 1592 play. I keep returning to *Faustus*, in part because it does something hundreds of video games and horror films like to believe they invented; it implicates the viewer, by delivering moral damnation as entertainment. *Faustus* makes a pact with the devil in return for magical powers and knowledge; consequently, he brings these wonders to the stage for us to enjoy. It's only at the end, when Faustus is dragged off the stage to hell, that we have second thoughts.

Another reason to love *Faustus* is that, centuries before headlines about games, critics claimed Marlowe's play had driven some of its audience members mad. There was even a suggestion that real demons appeared on the stage, 'to the great amazement of both actors and spectators', breaking the fourth wall by revealing the play itself to be a summoning ritual.

In *Doom* you go into every level expecting to die, again and again, but you keep playing. Unlike the calculated addiction tactics used by games today – the loot crates, the dark patterns and behavioural design – *Doom*'s approach was relatively straightforward. Romero and his team wanted to make a game so fun that you couldn't stop playing it.

Perhaps the danger critics saw in *Doom* was not that its players would be sent to hell, but that it might teach us to *love* hell. Perhaps we would become too powerful by playing – hell-bringers, gods of tiny, violent worlds.

Romero said, 'It's funny, with my son, when he was probably around eight years old we talked to him about hell, and he asked, "Why would you send a bad person to a place where only bad people are? Wouldn't that be awesome for them, like heaven for bad people?"'

It's tempting to claim that *Doom* exists because we transcended traditional morality, but then, what are we doing in playing it but killing demons and battling the armies of hell? Instead, *Doom* pays tribute to hell as a cultural phenomenon, a story that changes with every retelling, every player, every mod. Hell is a game we play with ourselves, and moral panics emerge when one hell-narrative falls away and is replaced by another.

Create and destroy. Create and *be* destroyed, then get up and create again.

Hell is eternal. 'Of course hell is eternal,' Romero said, laughing, 'because that's the whole idea of hell.' That final scene works as a sigil launched in the name of creativity. The demons are loose. Where will you go, now that hell is everywhere?

CHASING LILACS

Brenda Romero

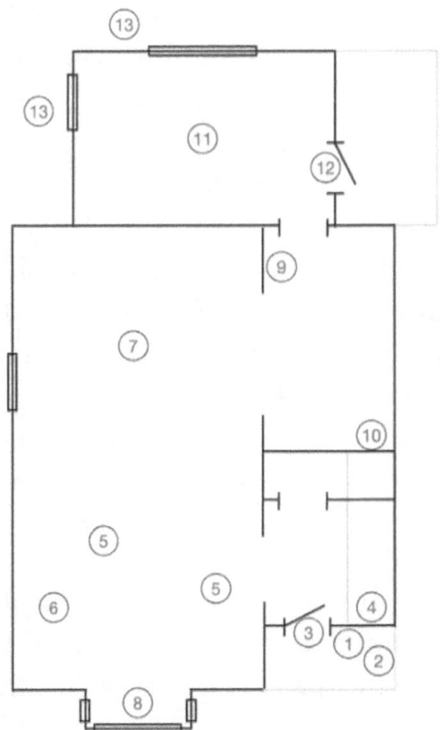

1) *House number.* The number 722 marks the address of the house on Montgomery Street.

2) *Front porch steps.* Ted sits here and practises his guitar for hours a day. If he makes a mistake, he tilts his head and says, 'Ah,' as if he's offended both Segovia and himself, and then he starts to play again.

   a) If you are four, you sit and watch him play. He stops playing Segovia and starts to play 'Salty Dog', one of your favourites.

   b) If you are ten, he asks you to sit as you walk up the stairs in front of him. He implores you: 'Listen, little sister. Listen.' You sit. The music of Segovia is the background music of your life, on the porch, in the living room, in his bedroom upstairs. You ask if he can play 'Bennie and the Jets', but he tells you that Elton John plays the piano and that song isn't really meant for guitar.

   c) If you are fifteen, you sometimes decide to skip the steps and walk around on the other side of the car towards the back of the house so you don't have to listen to Segovia or whatever he's playing. Shouldn't he have mastered it by now?

   d) If you are twenty, you are visiting home. You think of your brother, moved to Hawaii, and hear his music, even if he is no longer there.

3) *Front door.* The space inside the front door can be called an entryway or foyer, but these words seem bigger than the space, so it is called 'the front door'.

a) If you are two, your father greets your older sister's date at the door. He hands him a lead pipe and says, 'Bend this, and you can take my daughter out'. The young man struggles with the pipe, fails to bend it, and hands it back to your father saying, 'I don't think it can be done, sir.' Your father takes the pipe, bends it in a U with his powerful arms, muscles worked hard by a lifetime of labour, and hands it back to the young man. Closing the door, he walks back to the living room and sits down in front of the TV. Your sister, mortified, races out the front door trying to explain her father's odd sense of humour.

b) If you are four, you walk out the door holding the index finger of your father's right hand. He is six feet four inches tall, so you stretch to reach it. Sometimes, he takes your whole hand and swings you back and forth on your walks to Swann's Grocery to get penny candy from shelves behind the glass counter.

c) If you are fifteen, you welcome your friends in to play board games. Tonight, it will be *Monopoly* with David, Kathy, Danny and Deb. At other times it has been Julie, Andy, Maureen, Patti, Mike and Chuck. Lisa and Lori, Carrie, Paul, Kathy and Karen. Deanna, Gokey, Sam, Tammy.

d) If you are seventeen, you wake to a bang and your mother yelling, 'Get out of here!' You rush down the stairs to the front door to see her standing in her nightgown and robe, her hair dishevelled from sleep. She is scared, breathless, and tells you to call the police.

4) *Stairs up.* The stairs are to your right as you walk in the front door. At the base of the stairs, there is a mirror.

   a) If you are three, you hear your father walk up the stairs, home from the night shift at the St Lawrence Psychiatric Centre, where he works in the powerhouse. He calls, 'Who's that sleeping in my bed!' You throw yourself under the covers and hide behind your mother, but your laughter betrays your location. He scoops you up into his arms and cradles you into your own bed.

   b) If you are thirteen, you bound up and down the stairs spelling out the name of your first boyfriend, one letter per step. You think this brings you good luck.

   c) If you are sixteen, you kick a hole in the plaster of the wall. Your mother gets you up at 5 the following morning to replaster the wall. 'You can have coffee when you're done.'

5) *Living room recliners.* There are two recliners in the living room, one green and the other rust.

   a) If you are not yet born, your father sits in the living room chair in the dark. The front door is unlocked, and the windows are too. A string of break-ins have occurred, and he waits for the burglar to come in. What the police cannot solve, he plans to solve himself.

b) If you are fifteen, your mother turns the channel to Johnny Carson at precisely 11 pm. She watches the monologue while drinking half a Genesee beer. When Carson is done, she caps the beer with plastic wrap and a rubber band and heads upstairs to bed. 'C'mon Brenda,' she says.

6) *Couch.* Your mother upholsters and reupholsters the living room couch so many times that you no longer have a clear vision of it in your head. The colours of autumn seem the most common palette: rusts, mustards and burgundies. It has two throw pillows on it and an afghan, which your mother also crocheted.

a) If you are three, your father lies on the couch, home from the hospital having had surgery on the varicose veins in his legs. He brought you a bag of goodies which you now bring back to him one goodie at a time: packets of jelly, salt, pepper and sugar, a plastic jug for water, spare bandages left over from the bandage rolls for his legs. You pretend to be a doctor and ask him, 'How are you, Daddy? Are you OK?' You put your hand on his forehead to take his temperature and wrap his arms in bandage rolls. 'Don't go anywhere,' you tell him. 'I will be right back'.

b) If you are four, your father lies on the couch, tired and feeling out of sorts from shovelling snow off Mrs Santy's roof. He falls from the couch to the floor.

c) If you are fifteen, you sit on the floor between the couch and the coffee table to do your homework while watching MTV. Your brother, home for a visit, shakes his head and complains that music is for the ears and not the eyes.

d) If you are seventeen, you sit on the floor between the couch and the coffee table and flip open a *Playgirl* magazine purchased from the corner deli. Your mother comes in, stops walking past, and gasps. She confiscates the magazine and tells you never to bring anything like that home again, how dare you.

e) If you are eighteen, you are away at college and do not see your mother as she sleeps on the couch listening for someone trying to break in through the front door.

7) *Dining room table.* A mahogany table and chairs are in the centre of the dining room. The table is usually bare, with occasional holiday displays for Easter, Thanksgiving and Christmas. In the spring, it becomes an altar for a procession of lilac bouquets.

a) If it is fifty years before you are born, the table is in another home. Dr and Mrs Redmond sit in its carved mahogany chairs enjoying their evening meal. They discuss getting a new dining set, having grown tired of this one and its matching mahogany sideboard. 'What will we do with this one, then?' Dr Redmond says. 'Give it to the gardener?'

Mrs Redmond suggests. 'He's been good to us, and I am sure his wife would appreciate it.'

b) If it is forty-seven years before you were born, the table moves to your grandmother's house. She polishes the mahogany tabletop before setting the table for Sunday dinner. She takes the Spode plates, also donated by the Redmonds, from the mahogany sideboard and sets the table for four.

c) If you are ten, your grandmother asks you to polish the mahogany tabletop and set the table for eight.

d) If you are fifteen, your grandmother has passed and the table is in your dining room. You play games here, *Monopoly*, *Dungeons & Dragons*, *Trivial Pursuit*, *Kismet*, and games you've made up. On New Year's Eve, you polish the mahogany tabletop and set the table for two.

e) If you are fifty-five, the table is in your home office in Ireland. On weekends, you polish the table and set it for one.

8) *Front window seat.* Four windows – two up front and one to each side – surround a window seat that no one ever sits in. It is home to Christmas trees, televisions or plants.

a) If you are not yet born, your father walks to the window and stands there in the dark, looking out at the empty street, hoping for the burglar to show himself.

b) If you are four, you crawl under the window seat and hide. You leave the doors open, though, because you don't want to hide in the dark. You fall asleep as you hold your Drowsy doll. Sometimes, you arrange pillows in there and pretend it's a fort.

c) If you are fifteen, the area under the window seat is stuffed with board games, some store-bought, some homemade. You pull them out on weekends to play with your friends.

9) *Phone.* Similar to the front door (3), the phone room is named for the object in it that has the most utility, a beige phone with a ten-foot-long spiral cord.

a) If you are three, your brother moves a piano, guitars, amps and a reel-to-reel stereo system into the room. He poses for a photo in front of the piano while holding a guitar. His hair is long and curly.

b) If you are four, your mother calls an ambulance and then the Seymours, where you're playing with Julie, your best friend. Mary Ellen, Julie's mom, answers. 'Keep Brenda over there,' your mother says. 'Something's happened.' Mary Ellen replies, 'Jean?' but by then your mother is off the phone.

c) If you are fifteen, you spend night after night talking with friends, one friend after another. You still remember their numbers by heart.

d) If you are seventeen, you call the police to report an attempted break-in. 'He had a knife,' you say.

'He was trying to get in.' The police ask if everyone is OK. 'Yes,' you say. 'It's just me and my mom here.' The police are on their way to investigate.

e) If you are twenty, you call the police to report an actual break-in. 'No, no one was here. My mom is visiting my brother in Hawaii.' The police are on their way to investigate. You look around and see evidence – drawers open, candles broken, papers on the floor.

f) If you are twenty-one, your mother calls a real estate agent to sell the house. She no longer feels safe alone here.

10) *Stairs down.* The treads on the stairs leading down into the cellar are old, worn and uneven. They reveal the age of the house no matter how carefully your mother hides it under coats of paint and wallpaper.

a) If you are ten, your mother sends you to the cellar to get her a can of beans from a wall shelf hallway down the stairs. Ascending, you must juggle the need to turn the light off – the cord is hallway down the stairs, too – with the need to climb the rest of the stairs. Ahead of you, there is light in the phone room (9). Below you and behind you, there is dark. You know nothing is actually in the cellar, no monsters, no apparitions, but the fear always gets you, and you race up the remaining stairs towards the light.

b) If you are twelve, you stop to admire a nail in the stairs, a flat-hammered nail, from when the house was built. The official date given for the construction of the house is 1910. 'It might be earlier than that,' your mom tells you. 'That's the year the city gave all the houses if they were old.'

c) If you are eighteen, your mother sends you to get a vase for the spring lilacs. You walk halfway down the stairs, turn on the light, find a big vase, turn off the light, and try to walk up the remaining stairs. You imagine something grabbing your leg – nothing is going to grab your leg; there is nothing in the cellar – but you race up the remaining stairs.

11) *Kitchen.* The kitchen juts out into the garden. To your left, the appliances for storing, cooking, washing, preparing and cleaning form an L shape along the southern and western walls. A small maple table is in the centre of the room.

a) If you are four, your mother is cooking when she hears a cascade of thuds – boom-ba-boom – what she thinks is snow sliding from the kitchen's metal roof onto the ground below. There's another sound, though – a voice? 'George?' She hears a sound, low and guttural. 'George!' Your mother runs in from the kitchen to the living room couch (6) to find your father in front of it on the floor clutching his chest. 'George! George!' She kneels beside him. 'Oh my god!' He can't talk and moans in pain. She races for the phone and dials the ambulance. Hands tearing at his white undershirt, he grips his chest and arches his neck as he tries to pull air into his lungs. She cradles his head in her hands. 'They're coming, oh god, they're coming. Oh, George. It will be… they're coming. Honey, god no, please don't, my god George, no.' The police arrive first and wait for the volunteer ambulance, whose members must come first from their homes to the station and then from the station out to your father.

b) If it is the following day, the table is full of casserole dishes covered in aluminium foil, each carried to the back door by sad-looking people. Some give you a dish and leave. Others touch you on the arm or caress your face with their gloved fingers. One after another, you carry the gifts of food to the table, some still warm. You don't understand why people are giving food.

c) If you are six, your brother makes candles in the kitchen. To thin the wax and make more candles, he adds water to the pot. Within minutes the water turns to steam, sending hot wax popping, lava-like, out of the pot and onto the stove, counter, walls and ceiling. You run for cover under the maple table and scramble out towards the phone. Your brother braves the wax, shuts off the gas, and searches for a lid. You laugh until you cry, and your brother does too.

d) If you are twenty, you walk in the back door to check on the house to find the microwave on the kitchen table. 'Why,' you think, 'is the microwave on the kitchen table?' Then you see the Christmas candles broken in half, doors left open, their contents rifled. Room after room, drawer after drawer, it's the same. Someone has broken in.

e) If you are twenty-two, you find red wax under the cupboard closest to the stove. You leave the wax and hope it will still be there when you are old.

12) *Back door.* Unlike the front door, which has become the name for an entire room, the back door is simply itself, a passage between the kitchen and the back porch.

a) If you are three and it is the beginning of autumn, you open the door to see a deer gutted and hanging by its hindquarters.

b) If you are four, you open the back door to see a woman holding a casserole dish. Pursing her lips, she hands it to you and says, 'Give this to your mother, OK?' You're puzzled by this request, but agree, and bring the dish inside and set it on the kitchen table.

c) If you are twenty, you open the back door to search the porch where the burglar broke in. There, you find a receipt with Paul B's name on it, someone you know. You give it to the police, but they never make an arrest. Later, Paul B will be charged for a series of break-ins and attempted break-ins around town, all of them using a knife.

d) If you are thirty, you think of that receipt when you see Paul B at an AA meeting. 'Faith without works is dead,' the Big Book says. You work it.

13) *Lilacs.* In late March, the lilacs bud on two big trees whose leaves are visible from the northern and western windows. By April, the purple, lavender and white flowers cover the trees, and even the slightest breeze fills the house with their scent.

a) If you are fifteen, you wash dishes after dinner, study in the evening, sleep on the couch after school, all of it while breathing lilacs.

b) If you are thirty-five, you get a cutting of those lilacs from your sister, Mary Ann, who took a cutting herself when she moved away years ago. She brings it to you in Springfield, Massachusetts, and you plant it in your backyard, watering and willing it to grow and survive. In the spring, it rewards you with two leaves. When you move to Savannah, Georgia, a climate too warm, you leave the plant in Springfield to grow. You hope it makes it.

c) If you are forty, you beg your sister to send you some lilacs to Savannah. You just need to smell them. You offer to pay for overnight delivery. She thinks it's a ridiculous request, and it is, so she never sends them.

d) If you are forty-five, you ask a jewellery artist you admire to make you a lilac necklace with one flower darker than the others so that you might remember your mom, your home, and the scent of lilacs that filled the house on a spring day.

e) If you are forty-seven, you purchase four lilac trees to grow in your garden in the mountains near Santa Cruz, California. You get a few branches every year, never enough for a bouquet, but enough to tide you over year to year. A gardener asks if you are willing to take a large lilac tree from another client. 'Yes,' you exclaim. 'Yes, of course.' You hope for bushels of lilacs in your future.

f) If you are forty-eight, you stand in the garden taking a last look at your lilac trees. In the driveway, movers place boxes in a shipping container bound for Ireland. You cannot take the trees with you.

g) If you are fifty-two, you back out of the driveway of your new house in Ireland and are surprised to see a single large lilac bloom on a low bush. You stop your car in the centre of the street, park it sideways there. You rush to the bush, cup the lilac in your hands, and breathe deep.

TO WANDER, TO STOP

Chandrika Narayanan-Mohan

I am sitting on a bench, surrounded by plush trees in shades of pink and yellow and green. A colourful vista spreads out from below my feet, of soft grass, stone steps, gardens and ponds and a small lake sheltered by an enormous willow-like tree drenched in white blossoms. In the near distance is a charming house situated in the middle of a clearing, jaunty and cheerful, inviting. I put my hands on my knees, take a moment to brace for the weight of myself before pushing up to my feet. Music gently swells as I stand up, smooth out my apron, take in the view. I sigh, a heavy sound.

At the same time I am sitting on an armchair in my home. My legs are stretched out on a footstool, and I am tucked into an electric blanket, facing the windows so I can see the fresh buds of green exploding from the trees outside. A neck pillow props my head up, allowing me a more comfortable view of the Steam Deck screen resting on my belly. My hands are on the controls, positioned to move the version of myself on the screen off of her bench, down the steps, towards the cheerful building. Her name is Alta. Alta is a fighter who has never lost a battle in her entire life – until now. Horrified by her failure, she attempts to train more, be better, only to find her body keeps shutting down. She is broken, damaged, pushed beyond the brink by her own internal engine, by a voice that tells her that to stop, to pause, to rest, would mean certain death, certain failure. To find answers, she sets off into a forest in search of a renowned former champion who might train her back into her old self. However, every time she tries to begin the journey she collapses, waking up on a bench in the middle of nowhere next to a kind, calm, jolly creature who runs a tea shop in a magical clearing. He offers her time and space to recover by inviting her to run the teashop, which she reluctantly accepts. Stuck here in this colourful paradise, Alta is forced to stop and figure out why her body and mind have failed her, gently revealing painful memories she has locked away for so long.

The game is *Wanderstop*, created by Davey Wreden of the cult-status game *The Stanley Parable*. But *Wanderstop* is on an entirely different planet from *The Stanley Parable* and Wreden's games that came after it: it doesn't have the gritty edge of cleverness to it, where existential absurdism flips with every turn down a corridor. Together with indie-hit game *Gone Home* creator Karla Zimonja, the team at Wreden's Ivy Road studio have created a cosy game, intended to evoke peacefulness and relaxation, while still asking difficult questions or, more importantly, making the player face difficult answers about perfectionism, obsession and burnout.

I came to this game looking to play something beautiful and accessible with an interesting story that wouldn't take up too much of my time. I also liked the idea of playing a cosy game about burnout. It's been four years since I quit my full-time job in marketing and fundraising for an arts organization, and with plenty of time to recover from burnout and the terrifying internal drive that leads to it, I figured the story wouldn't hit particularly hard. I had already done the equivalent of 'running the tea shop': that was me leaving my full-time job in October 2021 to become a freelancer. I spent most of that month ploughing through all seven seasons of *Buffy* while horizontal on the sofa. I had already gone through the physical collapse part of the game: that was me across various jobs in 2014, 2015, 2016, 2017, 2018, 2019, 2020… The point is, that part of me is probably done and dusted. I've done my time already, when I was overworked while living alone during lockdown, lying on the floor in the middle of the day, feeling my face go numb when I made a mistake, silently crying during Zoom meetings or while writing emails because it saved time to cry *while* working instead of setting aside separate hours for it, while nobody noticed.

Also, the difference between me and Alta is that she seems to be inflicting this pain on herself, whereas for me it surely boiled down to only external factors. I had to work hard, because as a non-EU migrant my hard-won work permits depended on it, and if I wasn't the absolute best at what I did, I would risk being fired and therefore deported. Immigration restrictions affected every single part of my life for well over a decade, trapping me in jobs, in bad relationships and friendships, in homes I didn't feel welcome in, because in order to change those things I needed a new job with a new work permit, something near impossible to achieve for many years. And that paranoia wasn't unwarranted: I ended up in Ireland in the first place because I was forced to leave the UK at short notice in 2012 when they changed their own immigration policies. I buried a life I had built up over seven years to start again from scratch, on an island full of strangers.

See, now I'm wallowing in the past again, whining about things long gone. I have citizenship now, I live in a home that can't be taken away from me and I have full control of how I make my money, with plenty of free time. I have all the stability I need to fully put that burntout, terrified, broken version of me behind. So this game is great and all, but I really didn't think I would be affected by it.

Of course I was wrong. I found myself falling into the exact patterns the game was trying to identify as problematic for the character. After completing all the tasks the game assigned me, I was at a loss when I was told to just wander around and relax without something specific to do. I was taken aback when all my hard work was gently erased from one level to the next, to teach Alta (and in turn, me) that there is pleasure in gentle work for its own sake. As each level neared its end, I felt a desperation to stay where I was, to not change or move forward, to just exist peacefully tending the pretty garden, cleaning teacups, tidying up piles of leaves. 'Why can't things just stay the same?' Alta cries, distraught, and it echoes inside my own mind.

It's not the first time I've encountered the cosy genre and surfaced from it more emotionally devastated than expected. Last year I read *Legends & Lattes* by Travis Baldree, a cosy fantasy novel marketed as 'high fantasy – low stakes – good company' that isn't a game itself but was very much birthed from the world of fantasy role-playing games. This story is similarly about a fighter, an orc named Viv, who, in a moment of abject exhaustion during a quest, tired of chronic pain and the endless cycle of fighting, puts down her sword and stomps off into the distance. In a world full of taverns, she stumbles upon a strange new establishment called a 'café' and has her first ever cup of coffee. Invigorated by this new experience, she decides to trade in her sword for the espresso machine. I don't know what it is about barbarian-class fighters falling for the allure of serving hot beverages to strangers, but neither story holds back in its commentary on what happens when you achieve your dream, and then become disillusioned and broken by it. The final line of the book brought on an unexpected crying fit. This time, same as then, I assumed I was a lot more healed than I really was.

I encountered RPGs during one of the lowest times in my life. From 2014 to 2017 I had been working for a hospitality company, legally unable to quit due to Irish immigration policies, when I was invited to a game specifically for people who had never played tabletop RPGs like *Dungeons & Dragons* or *Pathfinder* before. A small group of us gathered in a dim kitchen to play *Star Wars: Edge of the Empire*. Despite playing numerous campaigns with different groups since then, that one session still remains the best I've ever played. In a phase of life where I was severely depressed and burnt out, working for exploitative employers and having lost the majority of my friends due to antisocial work hours, I was invited not to work but to play, to co-create stories with strangers who became my friends three hours later. Here the battle between control and freedom was finely balanced. I didn't have to manage these people, organize the meetup, clean up after, do any homework or prep. All I had to do was turn up and make a limited number of decisions within the confines of someone else's clear-cut rules. Using dice weirdly blew my mind at the time, just the concept of allowing such a degree of luck to propel your story felt so freeing. If you rolled a 1, it wasn't your fault. The word 'failure' wasn't a personal failing, it was a punchline that provoked laughter and camaraderie.

Almost a decade after sitting around that kitchen table, I was diagnosed as autistic. Looking back now it's obvious why RPGs were so soothing to me. I loved following the rules that someone else worked to set out, that everyone generally obeyed. The rules also expanded into the social contract for those evenings: people coming together for a common purpose, with no space for small talk or the ambiguity of socialising out in the wild. Over the years while playing *D&D* and *Pathfinder*, I also found catharsis in taking parts of my personality and turning them into the characters I inhabited: a cynical Rogue who trusted nobody, but was covering up a soft, privileged past; a necromancer sea-witch who was given a pass to 'act badly' because it was her best weapon and not something held against her; or a grieving monk playing out adventures to distract herself from everything she had lost.

But injecting a piece of yourself into a character can have its costs. During *DIE*, a sort of goth *Jumanji*-esque comic-turned-RPG created by Kieron Gillen, I created a character who was enraged because she was so horribly sad and isolated from the friends she once thought were on the same page as her. This was with a new gaming group after things went south with a previous one (*sigh*, girlies don't date your GMs, then move in with them, then have the relationship implode, and then lose your gaming group and all your friends). But *DIE* is no ordinary comic, or ordinary game, and is designed to pull deep-held feelings out of you, but without the potential of a happy ending. Which was the case for poor Malbec Bloodrage, my heartbroken wine-guzzling fighter who was the only one who failed a dice roll in the final scene, trapped in the world of the game forever as everyone else escaped back into the 'real world'. Ending that session genuinely shook me. I guess I was hoping to resolve that side of me, and instead, I trapped her in the same terror she was trying to escape from. Which weirdly enough did bleed out into the real world, because the GM of *this* game was also someone I was involved with, and when our friendship fell apart I was once again ostracized from a game group (say it with me again girlies, DON'T DATE YOUR GMS!).

Looking back at the characters I've created in games, it becomes even clearer why I am now attracted to games with heartbroken, exhausted, disillusioned women fighters. I might not have a table of friends to play with anymore, but these characters in books, or on my console screen, guide me through a story in a more gentle, safe manner, fully protected from the complications of relationships, miscommunication and the general mess of being vulnerable around a table with people I have no control over or insight into.

But video games aren't perfect either; they come with their own set of anxieties. When the only real variables are myself and the body I use to press buttons, and the brain I use to make decisions, it can end up revealing frustrating issues and, for me, disabilities. I was never good at video games because the connection with my hands and brain never quite lined up, which I now realize is likely a motor skill issue linked to my ADHD or autism. After fifteen hours of playing *Wanderstop*, my brain started to forget what A, B and X did on the controller, arbitrarily changing their purpose so that I started consistently clicking the wrong thing. When it comes to doing tasks that require focused motor skills, I don't tend to develop that muscle memory that comes naturally to others; my brain randomly derails it, injects irrelevant rule sets into the situation so I start making mistakes, which leads to frustration and dejection. I tried to play *Hades*, a game everyone said was fun and easy, but after eleven hours I still hadn't gotten past Level 2. I just couldn't seem to fall into an easy pattern with the controls, resorting to button-mashing and a total lack of strategy. Additionally, I have hypermobility issues, so it can be painful for my hands to use controllers for a prolonged amount of time. All this builds up into a horrible kind of self-loathing, attaching to an activity I was doing in an attempt to fucking RELAX.

This is where point-and-click games come in. Easy on the hands, a delightful challenge for my problem-solving mind and propelled by a singular compelling narrative with a limited game time, these suit me perfectly. My first ever experience of one was playing *King's Quest* on my home PC with my aunt next to me. I grew up with games because of my Burmese grandmother, who taught me how to play Gin Rummy, who played Carrom (an Indian game that's like a cross between pool and air hockey, where you flick a striker puck at smaller discs across a large wooden board into pockets at the corners) with me regularly, and played Mahjong with her friends weekly. My aunt was the daughter who inherited this side of her, at one time flaunting her Game Boy at me, an only child with not a console to her name. And so when she visited or stayed with us for short stints, my aunt would play games with me, slipping the *King's Quest* disc into the PC drive and sitting with me as we solved puzzles and inevitably got lost in the desert together. Unfortunately, she would always get bored and leave me to continue the game myself, which I didn't want to do alone (guess which side of my family my ADHD comes from). So, even though point-and-clicks are perfectly suited to me, because my journey with them began in a social manner, I still struggle to do them alone, enjoying them much more with someone by my side. My best friend Melissa, a dedicated point-and-click gamer since early childhood, introduced me to *Monkey Island* and *Broken Sword*, games we played together through school in Ankara, university in York and the years afterwards when we shared a flat in London.

I wish I could enjoy the solo aspect of these video games, but my brain craves the companionship of problem-solving together. I long for an activity where I can let go of all my limitations, physical, mental, emotional and social, where I can still enjoy the story and the mechanics and the catharsis of a game without the messiness of everything else that crowds my life. I want to be fully self-contained, fully autonomous, solitary. In a word, I want to be safe. Safe from the unknown variables that people and love and circumstance bring into a life. Safe from the external pressures and troubles of the structures my identity and body exist in, in any political and economic system. I long to enjoy things for the sake of enjoying them, without always focusing on what's absent or wrong.

I don't know if proud is the right word, but being a neurodivergent, traumatized immigrant is what I am and because it's led me to this moment, I guess I wouldn't have it any other way. Even though right now it's a bank holiday weekend and because, like Alta, like Viv, I don't actually know how to relax when things aren't expected of me, I am typing out this essay because I don't trust my mind and body to keep it contained in my brain until a more appropriate time. Even after a decade of therapy, multiple diagnoses and all the compensatory love and stability my child-heart could have ever hoped for, there is so much I can't seem to let go of. But as fighters should know better than anyone else, wounds take time to heal, and sometimes that part of you just isn't the same ever again.

As I play through the final moments of *Wanderstop*, I slow my actions. I walk instead of run through the grounds of the game, petting the weird little animals that live in the tea shop, cleaning up the last of the dirty cups, cutting away weeds. The game tells Alta to take her time before she says goodbye, that she can stay as long as she wants just to potter about and enjoy the peace, to drink cups of tea just for the sake of it. I make sure I'm happy with everything I've done. I survey the shop, take in all the plant pots full of colourful flowers, the picture frames full of memories from the game, the shelves stocked with tea and fruit harvested from the garden I have grown and tended to. The game is in golden hour, and I look out into the digital sun skirting pink clouds. I head towards the part of the garden that will take me to the end of the game, and I accept that this is the end of this story.

In the real world, I put down the controller, put my hands on my knees, take a moment to brace for the weight of myself before pushing up to my feet. The tinny music from the end credits continues to play as I stand up, look out the window, take in the view. I sigh, a heavy, but hopeful sound.

MEGA DREOILÍN

Donal Fullam

A committee of vultures sweeps the Dublin sky. Composed of landlords, investment funds and the political juggernaut known as Fianna Gael, they pursue a bloodthirsty quest to dominate all land and wealth, leaving death and destruction in their wake.

But hidden to them, an underground force unfolds its wings. Foretold by the Ancient Celts as An Dreoilín or Draoi éan – druid bird – the tiny wrens emerge as a fearless foe.

You must rise up to battle landlords, Gardaí and vultures casting a shadow over Dublin. But can you uncover the Mega Dreoilín, an ancient energy field within yourself and your allies, in order to face your final adversary?

Han and I first started talking about the possibility of making a video game in the Shop Fronts squat in Phibsboro. The squat was short-lived, but it allowed people to turn creative and political fantasies into reality. For some, this meant a space to play music, to sing and dance; for others, it was a vital organizational hub for Palestinian solidarity nights, Irish-speaking sessions, radical cinema nights and midnight plotting. For many, it was simply a space to exist in that didn't cost money. For Han and I, it became a space to conjure up a video game about the housing crisis.

The housing crisis in Ireland affects nearly everyone – over 15,700 people experiencing homelessness, workers struggling with unaffordable rent or mortgage payments, young people with no prospects of home ownership, and families unable to secure stable housing. Older people, those with disabilities and those who need specialized housing are acutely affected but often invisible, as people fall through widening cracks caused by failing systems and increasing economic inequality. The material effects are immediate and evident – delayed life milestones, increased financial strain, reduced economic activity – while the psychic effects are less obvious but no less oppressive. There is a feeling of doom in the air as the future for an entire generation becomes foreclosed, while the window of time needed to open it is shrinking and the dreaded spectre of homelessness looms. Han and I have decent, though increasingly precarious, jobs and neither of us could see any genuine prospects of home ownership, or even secure tenancy. Renting for decades means watching most of our incomes flow to landlords who own multiple houses, while we become ensnared in the permanent rent trap.

Some renters may eventually inherit property, but for most, the crisis seems inescapable.

The process of making *Mega Dreoilín* was a therapeutic mitigation of this depressing reality. It felt good to create a project that communicated the details of rent dystopia in a fun way, but it also consumed our lives for much of the year. Our social lives quickly became attenuated in favour of game development, which at the start meant weekly pizza/pint brainstorming, writing and design sessions at The Back Page in Phibsboro, just up the road from Shop Fronts. These sessions became social lifelines for both of us, but they were also crucial for the development process. Surrounded by Phibsboro's squatters, boozers and night owls, we outlined the story, and spent many hours whittling down a list of potential names. We are both big fans of Michelle Doyle, an artist and musician – whose music is in the game – and we were inspired by her *Super Gairdín* video work. The eventual name was a combination of 1990s gaming nostalgia and Irish mythology. After considering classic title conventions like 'Super', 'Saga' and 'Quest', we arrived at 'Mega Dreoilín', a nod to the Sega Mega Drive and 'Dreoilín' (Irish for wren) to tie into the Celtic mythology that forms the bedrock for the game's thematic elements.

Writing the story, creating the characters and brainstorming dialogue in the pub was half the work. The other half was teaching ourselves the software and design tools necessary to bring our pixelated golem to life. Han and I met through DIY punk – playing with bands in co-op spaces, organizing gigs in pubs and under motorway tunnels – and we brought that ethos into game development. Punk is about DIY and doing things without permission, so we taught ourselves the software needed to make it work and got stuck in. Game-making isn't magic. It's learnable skills, and all of the tools and learning resources we needed for *Mega Dreoilín* are fairly accessible, but also free. We began working in Godot, a free and open-source game engine, but we decided to switch to Unreal Engine because I had some prior experience with it. Unreal Engine is free for those earning under $1 million, and it features a suite of powerful and easy-to-use tools. We used GIMP (GNU Image Manipulation Program) to create pixel art and the Reaper DAW to edit audio and music.

Creating everything took about a year. After the initial brainstorming, research and writing continued up until the launch, using material from interviews we conducted with academics, musicians, artists, folklorists and squatters. We ended up editing dialogue up until the very last night – it took a lot of work to boil down long interviews into concise in-game conversations that retained the important elements we wanted to communicate, whilst also maintaining a good sense of flow. We settled on gameplay mechanics quite quickly – the genre staples of traversing platforms and defeating enemies with various weapons, including a hurl gifted by James Connolly. Blocking out levels and drawing a large amount of pixel art was labour-intensive, but it was very satisfying importing Guineys and the Cobblestone in and seeing the player character move around our blocky recreation of Dublin.

Underlying this process was an attempt to balance the bright, nostalgic tropes of 1990s platformers with a depressing story about evictions, mould and rentier capitalism. We wanted to create a playful space for people to engage with a grim topic, and encourage agency rather than passive spectatorship. This is what video games make possible: a space where players participate in the meaning rather than just observe it. This meeting point between aesthetic content and interactive form is where the expressive force of games as art can be found, an idea that, until recently, many dismissed outright. During the mid-2000s, the question of whether video games are art or not gained public attention when the American film critic Roger Ebert participated in a series of debates, and unequivocally argued that video games can never be art. In 2005 Ebert awarded a film version of *Doom* one star, and pushed back against the suggestion that viewers require knowledge of the game to properly appreciate the film. Now, he was correct – *Doom* is a terrible film, and knowledge of the groundbreaking 1995 game doesn't make it any less terrible, but Ebert went on to clarify his argument nonetheless, going even further by extending it to all games. He said,

> … to my knowledge, no one in or out of the field has ever been able to cite a game worthy of comparison with the great dramatists, poets, filmmakers, novelists and composers. That a game can aspire to artistic importance as a

> visual experience, I accept. But for most
> gamers, video games represent a loss of
> those precious hours we have available
> to make ourselves more cultured, civi-
> lized and empathetic. I remain con-
> vinced that in principle, video games
> cannot be art.

Ebert described video games as a non-artistic medium incomparable to more established art forms by explaining that 'one obvious difference between art and games is that you can win a game. It has rules, points, objectives, and an outcome', like sports. Connecting video games with sports was a way to suggest that they're not art, even if they're culturally important, but one problem with this explanation is that many established art forms also have rules – there are lots of different kinds of rule systems for music that we can use to play on our own or with other people, for example. The structures of video game rules don't have to be barriers to artistic expression, they can be expressive characteristics. The mechanics that Ebert dismissed allowed Han and I to portray the experience of precarity and the tenant's condition: constrained, but constantly moving, never settled. As we designed the game within these same conditions, leading up to opening night, the pressure mounted.

The final four months of creating the game were the most labour-intensive, and a self-imposed pressure occasionally strained our friendship. We were both working full-time, so game development took place during the evenings and weekends, usually in my dilapidated, under-construction room, squeezed between a bed, computer desk and a giant 1990s Sony Trinitron CRT we found on Adverts.ie. When we went to collect it, the seller threw in a 50 g pouch of Amber Leaf, which was odd but welcome. As the spring launch date crept up, deadlines and target dates came and went, and frustration sometimes mounted. Developing the game after long work days in a small, half-completed room was thematically apt, but did create the conditions for grievances to fester. We managed to channel our frustrations into grist for the game design mill, as we realized that our situation wasn't unique, but we needed to direct our anger towards more deserving adversaries.

Mega Dreoilín was to be part of a show at Pallas Projects/Studios, and the week leading up to the opening was a blur. Han was driving all over Dublin picking up props – couches, carpets, ashtrays – while I was glued to my screen, desperately trying to figure out why my level-loading function sporadically didn't work. We transformed the studio space into a 1990s/2000s-style rental accommodation, filled with the detritus of many lives half lived and on top of each other, constantly moving in, moving out and moving on. Like the game, it was a collage of mismatched objects: the couch and armchair were upholstered in different decades; the television sat slightly askew on a repurposed unit, framed by trailing wires and half-empty mugs; a clothes horse sagged under the weight of still-damp laundry in the middle of the room, because where else is there to dry clothes? Sallow light seeped in through blocked-up windows, gently illuminating cigarette burns on the couches and rollie butts in overflowing ashtrays. It was a space meant to be recognized and remembered, to draw players into the first level, based on my old house on Eugene Street, in the area formerly known as Rialto, now 'South City Centre' on MyHomes.ie.

While the last few weeks of development were punishing, it was also easy to slip into a rhythm as hours disappeared in front of the screen, the world outside barely registering. That state of absorption is the same altered focus that players often describe when they're inside a game. The psychologist Mihaly Csikszentmihalyi uses the term 'flow' to describe this psychological phenomenon, where 'people become so involved in what they are doing that the activity becomes spontaneous, almost automatic'. Academics, popular writers and players use Csikszentmihalyi's characterization of flow to describe the video game experience, which can be relaxing or intense, but always totally engaging. Many kinds of media, gameplay and other activities can induce flow, but video games provide players with an easy way to achieve this altered state of consciousness. Ebert focused on the surface realities that engage players: moving images, sounds, music and a high score, but video games are much more than the sum of these parts. They directly involve players 'in an active manner akin to ritualistic behaviour', through choices and challenges that create a sense of agency, affecting the outcome in some way.

The ability to engage with interactive gameplay mechanics and make choices that confer a sense of agency has fuelled the medium's immense popularity. Twentieth-century media artists like John Cage anticipated that interactive multimedia would foster a sense of independence and agency in audiences, but this democratic impulse has also been co-opted to express capitalism's managerial frameworks. Video games offer dynamic interaction, a series of choices that individualize experience – but these choices are always constrained within the parameters set by the game's designers. The illusion of agency is meticulously crafted, a hall of mirrors where every path is preordained, and what appear to be limitless choices are always foreclosed in favour of already defined outcomes. *Mega Dreoilín* was created in a cauldron of the same conditions it depicts – mould-ridden rentals, predatory landlords, violent evictions and the suffocating grip of rentier capitalism.

The idea was to evoke a time when homeownership still felt within reach for some, even as the foundations were crumbling. These are spaces we move through but never own, always precarious, never settled – and this is the essence of the platformer genre. Side-scrolling movement in one direction, always moving forward, never lingering, like the transience of the tenant's existence. We don't inhabit these spaces; we pass through them, chased by invisible forces seemingly beyond our control. The player, like the renter, has no real choice but to keep running, and to keep fighting for survival. The game's 1990s nostalgia is the hauntology of a generation forced into involuntary extended adolescence. Generation Rent, unable to reach traditional markers of adulthood, are lured into the comfort of regression – a tendency made visible in the constant stream of Marvel and superhero films, the endless sequelization of old franchises, and the incessant rehashing of familiar cultural touchstones. This generation in Ireland is the first since the 1940s not to experience higher real earnings than their parents, as living standards decline and rents skyrocket. At this point, the game of neoliberal capitalism has been played out and the choices have dried up. We can't choose where to live, where to work, how to conduct our lives – it's exploit or be exploited.

Opening night was stressful for me. I found it hard to watch people play, because I was nervous the game would crash. Thankfully it didn't, and I'm proud now that it wasn't a *Cyberpunk 2077*-style catastrophe. The game was stable and was also well received, with a lot of laughs and even some tears. Players immediately recognized themselves in the main character and the chaotic world of impossible housing choices. In Level 1, Ghouls and Ghost Estates, we traverse a dilapidated Celtic Tiger-era buy-to-let rental, battling mould monsters and encountering the double-barrel Anglo–Irish Ivan Cromwell-MacHugh, Dublin's mouldiest comprador landlord. The second level, Coombe Raider, brings players to Saol Eile, the Celtic Otherworld, where we meet the Morrigan, who demands an embrace of ancestral, collective resistance. In the third level, Bad Time Emporium, Dublin's stark inequalities are exposed, with James Connolly condemning Gardaí as tools of the ruling class. Connolly's spectral voice urges revolution: 'Unite, educate, agitate – the battle against landlordism is fought outside parliament.' The final boss – a giant vulture – can only be defeated by collective action, challenging the classic video game trope of the 'Chosen One'. The closing scene channels *Shinobi* and *The Terminator*, and exposes the state's deliberate fuelling of the crisis: NAMA land sales, tax breaks for vulture funds and a housing policy that only benefits the custodians of the market. The housing crisis isn't complicated – it's capitalism working as intended.

At an artist talk in Pallas, as Han and I played through the game, Rory Hearne – then an academic and housing activist, now a TD – spoke about Ireland's landlord-dominated policies and the far right's weaponization of displacement and disenfranchisement. He pointed out that 'mould in social housing causes asthma, chronic illness – landlords blame tenants instead of fixing structures'. He highlighted the game's timeliness: 'the far right twists Celtic imagery, but here, it's reclaimed for collective action', and praised the game's ability to humanize the crisis, saying that 'art is the most powerful way to communicate this. It's not just statistics – it's visceral.' The viscerality of *Mega Dreoilín* comes from a combination of factors: an altered state of mind induced through the flow of interaction; the recognition of mouldy Dublin rentals, recreated in a way that feels familiar yet strange – a kind of *jamais vu*; the possibility of killing your parasitic landlord; contemporary Dublin folk musicians colliding with ancient folklore; James Connolly in the clouds, alive in our hearts, along with a new world.

Do video games need to be classified as 'art' to matter? Maybe not. Maybe they're something else, and maybe they can be something else again when they are decoupled from the grinding mechanics of capitalism. They can be a space to practice for resistance, where the act of play becomes a radical reimagining of what's possible. Squatting demonstrates that alternatives exist, but there are many more. Direct action, self-management, communal living – ways we can refuse the rules of a rigged game, but they are choices that capitalism tries to erase. The only real choice left is refusing to play a game that was rigged from the start.

Em: We did it! We killed the head of the vultures! Now we can live in an Ireland that's free for everyone… right??
Sage: More vultures will swoop in to replace those we defeated. It's all driven by government policy.
Em: You're right. The whole rotten system has to change.
Sage: Viene una tormenta.
Em: What'd you say?
Sage: There's a storm coming…
Em: Tá a fhios agam.

TOMB RAIDER, REMASTERED

Anna Loughran

Distracted by the satisfying *swoosh* of rotating between items on the menu, I missed any alterations made to the screen's presentation. Instead, as I flicked between the sunglasses, passport and polaroid, I was preoccupied with a thought: was this how I remembered it? The sense of familiarity suggested it rang true, that loading into the game was close to the same experience as it was before, but something nagged. Was the familiarity I felt associated with *Tomb Raider*'s specific menu or with the sound itself, which could have been used in other games. Did that *swoosh* reside inside a box labelled 'assorted noises of the PS1 era' and, having been jumbled about a bit in the intervening years, become entangled and difficult to parse? How much does attention to detail matter when reconstructing the past? Do we need verisimilitude to make prior experiences legible?

After a few more rotations between the menu items, I selected the polaroid to load into Lara's home. Well, her *manor*.

Being slightly too young for the first game, I played the third more than any others, so the library the game loaded into wasn't quite as I recalled. However, its wood-panelled walls, chequered ceiling and dark-blue-paisley-patterned carpet matched the sensation of being in her home, of noticing wealth and being enticed by it. The remaster allows a toggle between modern and 'original' graphics by pressing the start button. By doing so, the changes made become apparent and are significant, with edges smoothed out, higher-resolution textures and additional assets: leaves filled in the trees outside; pillows were added to the reading nook; more portraits hung on the walls, including one of Shakespeare. Lara had changed too, with bangs either side of her now softened face and a long ponytail that swayed in line with her movement.

The game was automatically set to tank controls and I bumped into walls and struggled to angle her in the right direction as I headed towards the gymnasium downstairs for a tutorial on the game's mechanics. Once there, Lara's tutorial narration kicked in and suggested walking to an edge of a platform rather than running: with the former, she would not fall over an edge. This functionality is oddly quaint but vital to the precision needed for platforming sections. I spent around half an hour getting to grips with grapples, backflips, side jumps and rolls, with plenty of failed attempts. It was never easy, and often grating, to work the controls. Decades on, wrangling with the tank system was just as frustrating. The rules the old game lived by appeared outdated.

Fortunately, the remaster provided an option to switch from tank to modern or 'full analogue' controls. This, somewhat conversely, did not go much better. While the remaster maintained the game's 'original geometry', it meant the sensitivity and, for lack of a more technical term, wider turning circle of Lara's analogue movement led to a slipperiness whenever she moved across small platforms. Throughout this practice I frequently switched between original and remastered graphics, and running around in full analogue within the original's presentation soon started to jar. As if, by changing so easily between eras, by using the modern controls in the old style, I was collapsing the effect of time and starting to rewrite what memory I had of the game going in, those remnants of when I first played it in the late 1990s.

The PlayStation was a Christmas present that came with a wrestling game, a football game and possibly *Heart of Darkness* – a platformer with terrifying death animations. It was connected to the living room television in our terraced house on the Antrim Road. This was a few years into primary school, when it became clear that I did not fit in with other children. To improve that situation I was signed up to extracurricular classes such as karate, Irish dancing and horse riding. I didn't persist with any beyond a few lessons, finding it difficult to balance the complexities of social interaction and the pressure of having to do things a certain way. In some cases, there was the additional discomfort with an awareness of how my body was gendered by others. That is, of having to perform within another set of rules.

At least that is how I have come to understand and retell those experiences. I can't say with any certainty how much relation it bears to the actual experience of the child. What did they think? There is no way of knowing, but certainly the child did not have the ability to reflect and interpret, nor did they have access to language and frameworks of understanding that we gain as we age. What about how they felt? Did the bodily discomfort that I recognize now exist in the same way? Did they feel anxiety as I do now? I think there is some emotional continuity, but how do we read it? Why interpret the child through the lens of the present at all? Why strive to make ourselves readable? This issue of legibility is seen even in the choice of pronoun. Should I not speak of my past self as 'she'? Does not doing so undermine my being a woman? (No).

In the second season of *Transparent*, Davina shows Maura photos she'd had retouched by an artist so that her child-self presented as a girl. She notes how the pinstriped T-shirt had been changed into a pinafore and looks at the photo with a recognizable sadness, a grief for a past that wasn't. Maura decides to do this process too. Okay, I think. For some, that is healing. That is reclaiming the narrative of one's life. *I have always been a woman.* That is certainly the story medical gatekeepers want to hear, of a gender identity rooted in childhood, but such stories have been critiqued for contributing to the dominance of 'transnormative' narratives. Further still, such narratives map onto the diagnostic criteria for gender incongruence in adults, which means if one chooses to access healthcare you are required to dredge through memory and find moments that can evidence a medically approved history. This is not to say such narratives aren't based in truth, but rather that there is little scope for a broader range of experiences. What of those whose identity develops later in life, like those who had no language, no frame of reference or conception of transness because they grew up in oppressive environments? What of those who are nonbinary and need access to healthcare, but are required to present a narrative to doctors that matches a normative and binary criteria? The broader question is why do we have to make our pasts legible at all?

When I read over my own doctors' reports, the story they have captured is not a childhood I recognize. Key elements are present, but it is not what it was. More than half a decade later, the memories I used for that process have started to fade again. But now, when they do come back, I wonder how much they changed in the telling. If, for example, I retouched all my old photos and burned the originals, how much would that really change? At the very least, other people would remember that I did not look like a girl back then. In this case, multiple narratives would co-exist. Some closer to an emotional truth, while others more accurate in detail.

I continued to toggle between the remastered graphics and the original. Often this was to see what was altered, what assets had been added, like Lara's puffs of breath and a more 'realistic' representation of water. Much of this benefited the atmosphere, though not every change was welcome. The most glaring issue was the new lighting, a shift from the original's 'static' to a modern 'baked' system. The remastered lighting meant the environment's shadows appeared as expected: areas that would realistically appear dark, did so. Consequently, it became harder to navigate the level. The original's cruder system meant less variation and dim areas appeared brighter than they should. This change, as well as the additional foliage and recoloured rock formations, made it harder to see any signposted rocks that were designed to be climbed.

In both cases, the remaster's more naturalistic presentation jarred with the intended playing experience. To combat this, I would toggle to the older graphics for longer and longer periods. Then, after dispatching all the enemies in a section, I would switch back to the remastered graphics and run through the level to see items on the ground, which often blurred into the limited colour palette of the original. This process, of toggling back and forth between graphics, or adjusting controls to manage certain sections of platforming better, furthered a blurring of the boundary between past and present; there were times I forgot I was playing in the older style, and vice versa. To the extent that, after some time passed, I started to wonder how much the memory of my original playing would remain intact.

Take the moments leading up to the T. rex fight in the Lost Cavern. At this point, I was playing within the remastered graphics. Previously the cavern floor, due to its size and the older technology's limitations in rendering detail at a distance, was shrouded in black fog. When a smaller dinosaur attacked it emerged out of shadow to scare my eight-year-old self half to death. However, with enemies clearly visible in the remaster, they now lurched comically towards Lara. The sense of fear that came with her isolation had been lost in this translation. As in more recent games like *Breath of the Wild* or *Far Cry*, this emotional response was replaced with a problem-solving mindset. *Okay, the enemies are over there, this is how to best approach the situation.*

Similarly, I approached the platforming sections equipped with decades of gaming experience; for example I immediately recognized patterns of progression like finding key items to open a path to the next area. As such, I was able to approach each section methodically. But I had no such deeper understanding of game mechanics as a child. In that previous playthrough, I approached each new area with trepidation and often rushed through. Platforming was driven by a desire for discovery or out of sheer panic to escape wolves and dinosaurs. This shift created a more efficient playthrough, but not one that replicated the previous experience. It is, arguably, the emotive aspect that stays with us; it connects us to our past and makes what happened *feel* true.

In 2002, I was on a family holiday in Lanzarote. Ireland were in the World Cup and we spent a fair amount of time in bars to catch the games. Car horns erupted around the town whenever Spain scored or won. Dad rented a car, which we used to travel around the island, seeing the black beach or the volcano and taking the ferry across to Fuerteventura on a day so hot that, he said, you could fry an egg on the bonnet. One day, we visited a tropical park, which at least back then amounted to a maze-like enclosure packed with beautiful songbirds in cages.

I was deeply affected by what I saw, how cruel it seemed, and wanted to photograph what I could with a small Kodak I had for the trip. But instead of capturing them as they appeared behind a grid, I angled the lens through the bars to picture the birds as clear as I could. The resultant photos were blurred – lighting being a constant issue with the old compacts – and only highlighted the sorry state of each cage.

When I have tried to write about that experience before, I couldn't help but wonder if I was upset out of sympathy or empathy. Surely, as a child, I related to the birds' lack of autonomy. Such a reading would fit within that desire for narrative unity across a life. But there is no way to know what I was thinking – the mind of the child is beyond reach. Maybe I just wanted the photos, when looked back upon, to elicit joy instead of sadness. Maybe I just thought the bars were ugly.

I can't but read the past with the biases of who I am in the present, but the question is how much I lose or indeed create in the remembering. How much, to paraphrase McKenzie Wark, do I edit memory as I have edited flesh. If I can't help but reimagine the child's intention, I can at least root any such reconstruction in an emotive truth: seeing the birds made me sad. Similarly, if the replication of a past playing experience remained out of reach due to changes made to the game, or the inability to enter the mind of the child I was to play it again, what perhaps remains consistent was the sense of playing it.

Venturing through the dimly lit caves, clambering up a series of rocks to an unseen precipice, or sliding down an incline into an unknown area, all worked to emphasize Lara's isolation, of there being mystery and danger around any corner. It is exciting, and yes, an escape. Back then, I escaped from a difficult home life and being bullied at school. I stayed inside a lot because I found it too hard to cope with other people and being made to feel unwanted. Now, I escape a truly dire political environment that has resulted from the recent UK Supreme Court ruling on *For Women Scotland Ltd vs The Scottish Ministers*, which in effect has led to calls for trans people to be treated as their sex as assigned at birth. It is a sordid mess that has led to such anxiety that I leave the house less because of the headache that comes with ensuring anywhere I go has a safe place to use the bathroom. So sure I may approach *Tomb Raider* from a more intellectual position now, but those emotions, and that emotional need, are a connective tissue to the past.

Of course, another connective emotion is frustration. Oddly, this was also a delight in playing the game: despite its linearity, it is hard to know what you are meant to be doing. This came to a head in the second level, St Francis' Folly, when Lara had to negotiate up various pillars of different heights to reach a new area. The modern controls fell apart within the confines of the original game's 'grid system', and after a few (dozen) attempts at trying to line up a jump from a small ground-level platform to leap and grab a pillar, I decided to switch back to tank controls. The buttons remapped, and the camera became slightly more fixed, requiring some brief adjustment and use of the 'look' button, which fixed the camera to match Lara's eyeline. With these changes, it was easier to line up a jump, as the tank system enables Lara to sidestep and adjust her position with greater accuracy.

More helpful still was the backwards leap omitted from the modern controls. Each small platform is a box within the grid, and the leap covers the space of the box. Subsequently, Lara can perform a running jump within this distance. In practice, this makes negotiating tighter platforming sections easier, given the game was designed around them. I managed to climb the pillars, but instead of heading for the next area, I jumped to a small balcony that led into a dark room with various inclines: a platforming challenge that suggested a secret lay ahead.

After several (dozen) failed attempts, I caved and searched for a walkthrough guide to figure out what I was doing wrong. The writer laid out a precise method of holding the action and jump button for the leap onto the first incline, then releasing the jump button mid-air, which meant that, when Lara hit the incline, she flowed into a backflip, after which she would hit the next platform, leap into the air and grab onto the ledge above. This complex manoeuvre was at no point spelled out in-game, and yet this made it all the better. I was brought back to pouring through gaming manuals or magazines for hints, tips and cheat codes: small details of a 1990s gaming life.

I have been working on poems about childhood and part of the process is reading in public and seeing how an audience responds. I don't anticipate people will connect with the emotional undercurrent around gender – though it is nice when they do – but hope they will on more common ground, like complex family dynamics or feeling different from other people. What is most surprising, then, is when people respond strongest to details – images and sounds and smells that spark their own memory.

The wrangling of my past into a medicalized narrative had served a purpose, but it started to overwrite my own understanding of childhood experience, which was, for the most part, of a lonely and confused child who was bullied and looked to escape. Gender was there, in a messy and incoherent way, no doubt worsened by the lack of role models and language available at the time, but it was not the totality of experience. The child's emotional landscape was narrowed, their view of the world sidelined for narrative continuity.

To undo this work and try to broaden those memories of childhood, I focused on writing about details: conkers, greenfly, football stickers, toys. By trying to reconstruct why those details mattered to the child, I began to strip away the desire to interpret everything through the lens of the present. Sometimes things fascinated me because I was a child. I liked shiny stickers and wanted to collect more because I was jealous of other people's collections. I was fascinated by insects and the natural world, like most children, because it was new and I was closer to that world. I can't say with any certainty how true any of this writing is, but what does that mean anyway? Unlike a game, there is no fixed version to refer to. However, through this process the child was freed from the medicalized narrative imposed on them. There are thoughts and feelings that will be out of reach, sure, but the continuity between past and present became clearer. Similarities in what I did and didn't enjoy, recurring patterns of behaviour, anxieties that persisted over time. By attempting to understand the child on their own terms, I started to accept the past for what it was: a thing not to grieve but to learn from.

Before finishing up for the night I loaded into Lara's mansion in *Tomb Raider II*. I was welcomed by the clattering of teacups on a metal tray as Lara's butler watched on while she weighed up the obstacle course ahead. By this stage, I had developed a feel for tank controls and managed the course with ease. As a child, I probably spent more time perfecting a run in the obstacle course

and platforming around inside the gymnasium than playing the story. I suspect this had something to do with the
game being too difficult and a bit scary.

As I ran around the obstacle course, climbing frames
and crossing a zipline, toggling back and forth between
graphics, it was clear that it was impossible to recapture
that prior experience. There are aspects of the child's initial playthrough that are lost completely. Did I play in the
evening, or weekends only? Did I persist with it to prove
that I could handle more adult games? And what about
Lara? How much did I envy her athleticism versus my
own discomfort? How much did I see myself in her? I
have no idea, but I wanted to play as her more than any of
her contemporaries. This was not an intentionally made
connection, in comparison say to reading books about
other trans women now; I was not looking for representation. There was simply a need that I wanted to explore.
How much value is there in reading that child's experiences through who I am in the present?

There is a limit to how legible we can make the past,
because nothing is fixed. Our memories change and
evolve with us. Maybe a goal of these remastering projects
then, beyond the profit that can be made from nostalgia,
and the comfort they can provide in distressing times,
isn't just to preserve the past but to remind us how we
used to feel. The child I was had a greater range of emotions and experiences than the limited scope accepted by
the diagnostic process. To get to this truth has required
rewriting an already rewritten past – a re-making.

SO LONG NERDS

Paul Whyte

And that's what art is meant to be about – rescuing people from the fear of death and the fear of life…
> – Genesis P-Orridge,
> BBC interview, 1986

There is a moment in developer Rockstar San Diego's acclaimed 2010 open-world western *Red Dead Redemption*, where you – navigating through the game-world as main character John Marston – cross the open throat of the San Luis River and enter into Mexico. After a brief cutscene on the banks of the fictional Nuevo Paraíso, you are free again to roam this newly unlocked area of the sandbox. River at your back, and unknown territory just over the hill, you mount your horse and follow the track ahead. As you mantle the first hill, ready to regard this new landscape, carrying with you the weight and experiences of Marston's many trials to date, the thready, nylon heartbeat of Swedish songwriter Jose Gonzalez's 'Far Away' begins to play.

Until this point in the roughly four hours of a twenty-five-hour experience, music has fit the setting pretty evenly, a serviceable mosaic of the game's cinematic influences: Ennio Morricone's most well-known soundtracks, co-piloted by the discordant, psychedelic guitar tones of those 1960s westerns that your dad falls asleep to on a Saturday afternoon.

Gonazalez's vocals here are so out of place, yet somehow in harmony with what is happening on screen, that you can't but feel an elevation is taking place. The Mexican landscape reveals itself with a textured, arid beauty. An environmental art direction that is not exactly photorealistic, but instead a similar summary of cinematic influences as its soundtrack. Immersion is a tricky thing. It seems easier to know what might break it than what will sustain it. This sequence, though immersion does suffer for a beat, elicits an appreciation for the choice – and though you can feel the subtle coercion, the choice is so on the money that you can't help but just go with it.

Depending on the time of day you reach it, every player's first steps in this territory will be slightly different. For some it will be the dead of night, where the sky-box of stars will be your only light until dawn; for others the sky will moan with thunder and crack briefly with gin blossom lights. For me it was late afternoon, sky ambient white, slowly oxidizing towards a satin dusk. The path splintered, a cankered and rolling landscape gave way to the mood of the river, and then all at once I was in an open field galloping towards the horizon.

It's a wonderful (if emotionally cynical) moment, calculated through particularity and the illusion of circumstance; so many elements and covert little nudges seem to have to conspire in order to catch you inside its vision. How you let it happen to you, though, is your choice. You can stay still and watch the rhythms of a temperate earth, or dismount and wander off towards a distant tree line, painted in the tobacco grasses of the steppe. Wildlife will blink away from you, snakes will hiss, your spurs will bell and clink off earth as you wander, all soundtracked by that dysphonic Swedish vocal, which will eventually whisper away and leave you with just the sound of the wilderness for company.

The placement of the song, and its setting, has rendered something of a surreal emotional response from gamers. When I browse through the comment sections of the sequence's many appearances on YouTube I note the responses are overwhelmingly positive, and at times quite touching. Testimonials of time and place. Of loved ones lost and depression thawed if only for a minute.

I wonder why – unlike many of the other moments that have stayed with me – this one isolates itself as one that I remember without time or sensory indicators. I have no idea what else happened in my life in 2010. When

I search my camera roll for photos, the only picture that seems to have survived from that year is a screengrab from the television show *30 Rock*. Tina Fey's Liz Lemon is staring through a restaurant window. The dialogue caption simply says, 'Nerds.'

Next, I pull up a list of major game releases from 2010. *Halo: Reach* came out that year, as did *Mass Effect 2*, *Fallout: New Vegas* and *Metal Gear Solid: Peace Walker*.

The sensory equipment begins warming up – I start to remember playing *Halo* under the compact fluorescent light of my parents-in-law's spare room, where my wife and I stayed while we saved our house deposit. I can hear my friend's giddy voice on the phone, discussing the opening scene from *Mass Effect 2*. Then my stomach turns a bit sour. I see myself playing *Peace Walker* on the PlayStation Portable, sitting in a sterile room inside St Vincent's Hospital, waiting for my father-in-law to finish his chemotherapy. I played the entire game from start to finish in these waiting rooms. All twenty hours of it.

That would have been in February of 2010, so in May, as he began to recover, I would have reached the Nuevo Paraíso steppe, and heard that song play for the first time.

This sequence is often featured on those endless lists of 'gaming's greatest moments' you find online. Though rarely at the top. Most of what you find on these lists will belong to the big reveals and twists: sucker-punch deaths and enormous challenges conquered. What is striking about the resonance of this moment is that this sequence has no bearing on any of the usual narrative elements – it doesn't propel the plot or reveal much of anything at all. On paper it's a musical interlude to set mood, and to bookmark the player's arrival in a new area. A device Rockstar has used time and time again – one that stands in contrast to the menagerie of over-pronounced characters that drive many of their narratives.

Even here in Nuevo Paraíso, I am ferried across the river by what can only be described as the worst Irish character in any video game, ever. His name is literally *Irish*, and his only real traits are that he is a bumbling, morally defunct drunk who ends up misadventuring himself in the face, while sitting on the toilet. Yet their games are filled with these moments of cinematographic atmosphere. The physics of weather and light, moderated by music, mood and art design, are most memorable above even the most cartoonish violence or schlock humour. At gunpoint I couldn't recount for you the plot of *Grand Theft Auto: Vice City*, but I do remember the first time I got into a vehicle. I can recall the suffocation of air pressure in a post-storm sky, the blue-dark of the alley and the heat of the internal lights as the bass riff to Michael Jackson's 'Billie Jean' kicked in. I can see the loose pages of newspapers kicked up about the bonnet, and the pitch of tyres on wet concrete as I took off towards the city.

When I poll my gaming WhatsApp group for everyone's most poignant moments in gaming I am pleasantly surprised by the engagement. The group was created in 2016, originally built around the co-operative 'looter-shooter' *Destiny*, where in order to participate in certain end-game activities, at least four players are required to play together at a time. Since then, we've solidified friendships, attended each other's weddings and organized milestone birthdays together.

The moments start coming in at speed. There are some, like encountering Measurehead in *Disco Elysium*, or the 'would you kindly' twist from *Bioshock*, that are more narrative driven. While others come out like mini-soliloquies over lost friends: mourning their time lost wandering the Capital Wasteland in *Fallout 3*, or experiencing the lights and sounds of a stormy night on the Hudson in *Metal Gear Solid 2: Sons of Liberty*.

Over the next few hours, more experiences come pinging through, all narrowing towards a common thread. One friend shares a rabid competition that took place in his secondary school over who held the highest score in the 100-metre dash in *International Track & Field* for the original PlayStation. As he tells it, the competition became so serious that, when someone was caught lying about their score, an independent adjudicator was chosen and, from then on, that person would need to be physically handed a memory card before any score could be confirmed. He speaks of this appeal for paternalism with a certain pride. It's as if his final leap through the blood-brain barrier into fantasyland couldn't be complete without the cold presence of the state. Dark stuff.

Overwhelmingly, the moments that come through are ones of fraternity and friendship. Brothers locked in intense silence as they attempt to defeat Goro in *Mortal Kombat*; those late-night raiding parties in *Destiny* and the elation of victories shared; or that time in school when someone discovered they could install *Quake II* in the computer room, and somehow got away with hosting LAN parties every lunchtime throughout transition year.

It occurs to me that these memories have all been bound in time, to spaces of a certain intimacy, to the bedrooms and living rooms of our childhoods, to the moments and places that make a life feel safe enough to be lived at all.

We are often at our most vulnerable when we play them, dressed down without footwear or formal attire. Even outside of our own homes or the homes of friends, we are shellacked into headphones, trying to disassociate from the crush of a busy tram.

I wonder if intimacy is integral to the experience, or do I play video games in the hope of experiencing it? This is perhaps what I sensed as I rode through Nuevo Paraíso for the first time and had myself a little cry as the song hit its chorus, and why this memory stayed while everything else left. I felt the intimacy of expression. A memory card shared with an independent adjudicator. An acknowledgement. Of a hard journey ending, and a new one started.

In 2013 my eldest son Noah was diagnosed with a severe allergy to milk protein. It is so severe that he requires an

EpiPen. It's so intense that if he eats a piece of steak cooked medium rare the protein similarity will confuse his immune system, which will send histamines to his tongue; his vessels will open to allow blood into an injury that is not there, and his tongue will itch and swell. We learned about his allergy when we moved him onto baby formula. He was only a few months old.

At first it was an inconvenience. He would be sick if he drank milk, so we had to switch out his formula to a grey, soil-smelling substitute. Then, when he was eighteen months old his cousin innocently touched both his ice-creamy hands against Noah's face. When I handed him to the nurse in Crumlin Hospital both his eyes were completely swollen shut and his face looked as though it had been bitten by a rattlesnake. I had an anxiety attack and vomited into a really small sink and then possibly had a slow-release nervous breakdown that lasted a year. After the antihistamines began to close the blood vessels, I sat with him and we played *Angry Birds* on my iPad in the hospital bed. Two days later, when I went back to work, my wife sent me a video message from him, asking if I could come home early and play *Angry Birds* with him. So I did.

As is often the case with allergies, asthma became a factor. When he was younger and slighter, chest infections would set him back in his tracks, and with him in this state I couldn't bear to sleep without a part of my body touching his. One December Noah was so sick we lay on the sofa together for an entire weekend, day and night. I remember the indigo of the evenings and the displacement of the sofa to make room for the tree. This same weekend *Super Smash Bros: Ultimate* was released on Nintendo Switch, and though he was nauseous and terribly wheezy we played together all through the weekend, slowly but surely unlocking every character on the games roster. We lit the fire at night to keep us warm and stayed up unreasonably late. After each victory we got closer to completing the set. *A new foe has appeared!* If you've seen this meme online – this is where it comes from. Through the night he would wake, in need of his inhaler, and would tangle into me afterwards and ask if he could play some more, and I would let him.

This is my favourite gaming moment. It's actually more than that – it's one of my favourite moments from being alive at all. Perhaps that's sad, or wrong – I don't know. But there is something in the untranslatable privilege of being able to care for your child, the closeness, the cortical warmth, and the minor elation of finally unlocking Link from *The Legend of Zelda* that I suspect I will long for, in whatever lucid moments I have left, at the end of my life.

As he gets older Noah's allergy episodes are becoming more severe. He will need to keep adrenaline with him probably well into adulthood. One Sunday he was at his cousin's house and I went upstairs to play some Xbox alone. The console auto-resumed inside his *Fortnite* locker. I could see his collection of character skins and emotes, all his purchases and achievements connected to the sum of his actions in the game. A dark thought crept up on me. I saw what this locker's significance could mean to me if the worst possible thing in the world were to happen. This was a record of him, as pathetic as it probably seems – there he was. His choice of username, his choice of dress and the music he liked to dance to. I reminded myself that we leave many records behind after we leave, and that this is simply a newer one. No need to add significance to just one, unless you want to assign it to them all. Perhaps we should.

All three of my children have accumulated a similar store of virtual objects. They hold some of them as dear as any toy they own in the real world. It's a constant struggle as a parent to maintain a healthy equilibrium between what they should be playing, how long they should be playing it and how much real-world money they should be allowed to invest into their favourite game world. Of all the worlds that they enjoy, one stands above the rest: somewhat inevitably, this world is the world of *Minecraft*.

Developed by a single person and released to the public in 2009, *Minecraft*'s ascension to cultural ubiquity had been well predicted by the time Microsoft purchased it along with its developer Mojang Studios for a reported $2.5 billion in 2014. In retrospect, they got this for a steal.

Since then, the game has reached an estimated 600 million unique players. Yearly profits fluctuate, but in general it makes anywhere between $200 million and $500 million a year. This is not counting merchandise or, indeed, as we saw in 2025, a film release that will have earned about a billion dollars by the end of its first twelve months of release. On YouTube, videos containing

Minecraft have reached over a trillion unique views. *Minecraft: Education Edition* is now used in over 40,000 schools across 140 countries.

In the area of childhood play, the game has now acquired an equivalence to something as fundamental to play as the crayon. It is a game that is so simple in its concept that even a child can understand it (you build things with blocks), while being drawn in a vibrant aesthetic that seems tailor-made for a toddler's eye.

Given its status in our home, the excitement around the release of *A Minecraft Movie* was mega. As it turned out, my eldest son and my daughter would be seeing the film as part of a school trip, so it would be just my youngest son and I attending the first (of multiple) screenings together. The film stars Jack Black as *Minecraft*'s protagonist, Steve. Apart from wearing a similar set of dark-blue jeans and light-blue T-shirt, no effort has been made on Black's part or the film's to make him look anything like Steve in the game. This fits with the rest of the film, which barely has a plot and seems mostly to have been improvised in front of a blue screen. The whole thing feels like it could have been filmed in an afternoon.

My children adore it.

Approximately halfway through the film's runtime Jack Black and friends enter a village, stopping to acknowledge a pig that is, for some reason, wearing a crown. 'Is he some sort of king?' someone asks.

Jack Black pauses and says, 'No. That's a legend.'

My son cupped his hand against my ear and, in his adorable lisp, whispered to me, 'That's Technoblade! The wootuber. I love him.'

The name Technoblade was already in there somewhere, packed into whatever partition I use to keep all the online news I consume in a year – but I couldn't recall much else about him, apart from that he was a YouTuber who produced *Minecraft* content, which included one very popular video with MrBeast.

That evening I went down a Technoblade rabbit hole. I'm not sure I will ever come back out.

Technoblade's real name was Alex. Alex first began uploading videos when he was only ten years old. He was particularly skilled at PvP (player vs player) games. Some of his earliest videos were simple Let's Plays of *Roblox* and *Team Fortress 2*. His avatar was, of course, a pig wearing a crown.

During a video celebrating his channel reaching one million subscribers, Alex admits that he only pivoted to *Minecraft* content after seeing the game's surge in popularity. He describes his channel's change to *Minecraft* as 'playing YouTube on easy mode'.

Leaning into his strengths, Technoblade grew his audience by participating in highly competitive *Minecraft* PvP communities like Hypixel, where popular mini-games with bespoke rules had been created for competitive play. Technoblade had a skill level that approached savant, and began to rise in popularity due to his channel's mix of high-level strategic play and his quick, dry-witted voiceovers that included his signature victory cry: 'Technoblade never dies!'

His fans appear to have loved him with a genuine ferocity, and if you spend any time watching his videos (as I did) you will soon understand why. His voice is much richer and deeper than someone of his years should be. It is gentle and mature and filled with kindness. He is funny and inherently un-smug about his abilities, allowing fans to root for him without ever feeling punished or let down for doing so. He seems an underdog but almost always wins. There is a sense that he will never let you down.

At the height of his popularity, while holding over ten million subscribers, Technoblade vanished without trace or warning. It was the summer of 2021, and the Delta variant was at its peak. Many fans began to speculate that he had fallen ill with Covid-19. Then in August a video titled 'where I've been' appeared on his channel. Over the course of thirteen mins and one second, the YouTuber announced that, at just twenty-one years old, he had been diagnosed with sarcoma, a rare cancer that typically impacts the connective tissues between the muscles and bones.

The video itself is delivered in his trademark style, played out over gameplay footage. He frequently laughs not only *about* but *at* his diagnosis. He pauses to advertise his plushie range, makes jokes about the sounds he believes his tumour is making at him below his skin, and explains that he will not stop producing videos or playing video games while undergoing treatment. 'This is the safest place I can be right now,' he tells us.

Technoblade continued producing videos, taking only periodic breaks for treatment. And over the next twelve months, fans got somewhat comfortable with the idea that everything was going to be fine.

On 30 June 2022, after a short silence, a video titled 'so long nerds' was uploaded to Technoblade's channel. The video opens with a man Technoblade's audience does not recognize. He is holding a fluffy white dog, and is sitting against a white backdrop. This is Technoblade's father. He begins by telling us that Alex has died and that over the last few months, as Alex came to accept his fate, they had both discussed what to say in his final video. In the message, read by his father over a *Minecraft* gameplay video, Alex apologizes for pushing his merchandise so aggressively in his final year but is proud to reveal that he has raised enough money to send his siblings to college (if they wish to go). He tells his fans that he loves them and that, 'If I had another hundred lives, I think I would choose to be Technoblade again, every single time.'

In the space of an evening I watch the birth and death of Technoblade. I hear his voice break from child into teenager. I watch a role-play video of him pretending to be a character stuck inside a tree. I listen to him laugh at how aloof his doctors are being as they suggest he amputate his arm in order to survive. Even without a second arm, he posits that his skill level will only have been impeded by about 30 per cent.

I have a pathetic little cry as I watch his final video. Alex's pronouncement of being at cosmic peace with his ending, and that he would, if given the choice, endure the horrors of cancer treatment again a hundred times over, just to live this same life again, expresses the sense of belonging, intimacy and fraternity that this pastime lends many of us.

The story of Technoblade is viewable as sectioned chapters – paragraphs written in the language of Eternalism. I open his YouTube channel, and I can see the entire grid of his online life. I am an observer outside of time, scrolling the flat surface of the fourth dimension. Moments uploaded – to be used as a traversable ladder through the hypersurface of reality.

Though perhaps there really is only the one moment, as Special Relativity may well suggest – a single sustained moment, a diorama, loomed to the physics of light, and the technology used to receive it.

In this moment Technoblade never dies; his ending is just another pixel on the face of a temporal object. Rendered by forces unknown, using whatever instruments they have for shaping it. Mediums that draw us together, invisible spaces, where we gather to meet our people. Checkpoints, in the hyper-real.

Noah is at the age now where his gaming sessions are beginning to bump up against my own. Our attic has a television and comfortable chair set up in it and is quickly becoming prime real estate in the evenings. Often, I'll give up and let him keep playing with his friends until bedtime. Sometimes, when I place the headset on my head, the foam cups are still warm from his temples. His friends will deliberately join the voice-chat where my friends and I are busy barking orders at each other, demanding I let Noah come back and play. They've discovered that they can get a rise out of us and now every party-chat we create must be set to *invite-only*, for fear of an invasion. They are very proud of this and like to point it out to me when they call to the front door. It feels as though I am watching something new being born.

A new moment. For some new nerds to share.

YOUR JOB SUCKS? TRY WORKING IN GAMES

Úna-Minh Kavanagh

With a title like that, you're probably thinking I don't like the industry I work in. I do. But given the sheer madness involved in making games, it's a wonder how a single game (good or bad) gets made at all.

Here's a fact: growing up playing games does not equate to experience in the games industry. Many gamers say, 'I'd love to work in game dev', but if they had a front-row seat, they might realize that they'd rather spend time playing games than making them. Indeed, most gamers don't understand how games come to be. They don't see the hours of crunch, cancelled social events and constant back pain. They don't see the industry layoffs, the closed studios, the struggle to find entry-level positions. They don't see the fact that, in 2024, there were more layoffs in the gaming industry than in 2022 and 2023 combined.

And they don't see the utter disappointment in our eyes when no one seems to care about the thing we've worked tirelessly on.

But what they do see are the bugs. They see that one typo you thought you'd fixed at the end of a fourteen-hour day. They see the quest that doesn't quite make narrative sense because stakeholders demanded more 'content'. They see all the human errors and count them as simple, easy-to-fix issues.

And oh boy, do they tell you.

The final package to them is summed up as GAME TITLE – OUT NOW, followed either by scathing or glowing reviews. Done and dusted with no more to say.

I, too, had a sincere lack of understanding growing up. A gamer since the 1990s – still am – I was ignorant of the fact that games do not magically fall into one's lap (or into one's game library). I had a lofty vision of myself playing games all day to make them better. I was quick to form opinions on how I could do better to change a level or a plot point, but ask me how that would be achieved and you would be met with a blank stare. To work in games, you need at least a few things:

- The ability to accept feedback, good, bad or indifferent.
- The ability to accept that your game might not see the light of day.
- The ability to accept that your game might not make a cent.

- The ability to accept that some will actively dislike your game, no matter how many good reviews it gets.
- The ability to accept that, knowing how the industry works, you might end up hating games.

With those firm abilities under your belt, I welcome you to the world of games. I'm a producer, which, many of my fellow producers will agree, is one of the most under-appreciated roles in the industry (Quality Assurance [QA] being another). Most people don't know who the producers, writers or programmers were on TOP GAME NAME HERE, but they will know who the director is.

And no, it turns out, producers don't spend all day playing games.

So how does one even get into game development? Here's the good news: there's no set route. I certainly didn't take a traditional route. I'm an author who has a BA in Journalism through the Irish language, for goodness' sake!

To work in games, you don't need:

- A degree in games
- To be any sort of 'hardcore' gamer
- To start in QA

Some folks will claim that QA is the easiest way to start your game dev career. They're liars. For creatives, this is not what you want. Why? While QA works super hard, they have essentially no say in the game's development. Sure, you'll get to play the game again… and again… and again… But be prepared for monotony. Even for people with passion, burnout is quite common.

In my case, I took a leaf out of computer scientist Cal Newport's book, in which he advises you to be 'so good they can't ignore you'. I had a very specific set of skills. Random skills, yes, from years being a journalist, author, content creator and writer, but key skills nonetheless. I wasn't just a 'passionate' gamer, I was determined to get in.

My first real dip into the industry was through localization work during the Covid-19 pandemic. Localization is mostly translation work in the industry, but it also means adapting the product to suit the needs of a specific market, e.g. cultural references.

There was understandably a lot of 'downtime' during the pandemic, and while we all got to grips with restrictions, many of us headed online to play games. One such social deduction game, *Among Us*, took the world by storm. I was a Twitch livestreamer during that time, playing games in both Irish and English, and the more I played *Among Us*, the more I found myself wishing there was an Irish version. And so a group of folks, including myself, set to work on an Irish-language localization. Even though it started as a passion project, my role soon developed into a project manager position. It wasn't paid, after all, no one asked us to do it, but we were diligent about the work and wanted to fill in every line possible.

As the translation came to completion – or so we thought – I thought about how we could leverage it to become something more than just a fan creation, and so I set to work on reaching out to my network and the *Among Us* developers, Innersloth. I pitched the idea as so:

The Irish language is a minority language, not often seen in games. Innersloth would be supporting and releasing their first minority language into *Among Us*.

Most of the legwork was already done because we'd already translated hundreds of strings (spoiler alert: it wasn't).

With the backing of hundreds of fans too, back when Twitter was not fully a hellsite, Innersloth thankfully saw the value of my pitch and brought us on board to 'complete' the translation and, yes, we were paid. I say 'complete' because the *Among Us* Irish-language localization is still being updated today.

Since then, my team has worked on other translations, such as *Axyz* (2025), *Terry's Other Games* (2025), *VVVVVV* (2010), *Crowded. Followed.* (2025), and another unannounced game. Oh, and here's another tip: get used to referring to the thing you're working on as an 'unannounced' game and be prepared to reference your NDA a lot!

That was my foot in the door, no experience required. Like I said, you don't need a degree to work in games. With a taste for the industry, I sought my next opportunity with Die Gute Fabrik (DGF), a Danish company looking for paid writing interns. I applied using skills developed over the years as a journalist and author, i.e. writing, and completed their requested writing test. I made it to the final interview, beating over a thousand applicants, and met with the team; I felt pretty great about it.

I didn't get the role.

To work in games, you need one more thing:

The resilience to bounce back from countless rejections.

And so I did. I didn't get the role – so what? Thankfully, I was in no different a situation to the one I was in when I applied. I fell back on the career I had built with freelancing, and back to a series of financial unknowns. But what I did know is that I gave a great interview. A few months later, I got the call from DGF about another role they thought I'd be good at: Executive Assistant to the CEO. I took it.

While with DGF, I quickly moved from the position of Exec to Assistant Producer, where I found myself truly knee-deep in the world of games. 'On spec, on time, on budget', a common phrase amongst project managers, became a cornerstone of my lexicon. I also quickly learned that being a game producer meant that you wore many hats, and no studio had a consistent job description for what a producer even does. Here's my best stab at it with a million caveats.

A game producer oversees the entire process of creating a game, from concept to final release. Their job is to ensure quality and timeliness, and to stay on budget. They manage the dev team, coordinate with departments and act as a liaison between the higher-ups and the publisher. They can also usually step into many roles and take over tasks to alleviate some of the pressure on other team members. We're the people who must say 'no, that's not possible' to those who want more features and also are those who ideally try to empower the team to speak up and take ownership.

A producer is a juggler, dancing between internal conflicts that could run a project off course and a masseuse smoothing out the creative vision to meet agreed-upon milestones.

It is worth noting, though, that there are many types of producers in games, even within a single studio, depending on its size. Some studios even have both a producer and a project manager, and their roles can blur a bit. Others may have a technical and creative producer specializing in different aspects of the studio. So like I said, take all of this with many caveats.

I was good at my job. It was hard but rewarding, and we shipped our story-driven adventure game *Saltsea Chronicles* in 2023.

Remember the 2024 layoffs I mentioned earlier? I fell into that pool too. How did that happen? Let me explain.

During the early pandemic years, the games industry saw a surge in gaming as people spent more time at home during lockdowns. There was a sharp increase in revenue for the industry worldwide, and this led to studios being able to scale up and hire and hire and hire and hire. The knock-on effect was that, when the pandemic ended, there was an economic slowdown, which made it challenging for any company to secure funding. Thus, no new investments in new projects and no way to maintain existing ones. It was all too common to see publishers either cancel or delay their games and lay off game developers.

Just after I came back to work from celebrating my wedding in early 2024, I was informed that the company had to lay off the majority of its staff and go into hibernation. There was simply no publisher who was willing to fund 'the next thing'.

Your job sucks? Try working in the unstable games industry.

For me, it was time to muster up more resilience. Back to the drawing board. I knew I wanted to try to stay in games, and to do that, I needed to keep my skill set sharp. The tools and tech involved with making games are constantly in flux, and just like there is no set description of what a producer is, there are also no set tools that every studio uses.

But while I was upskilling, I was also spending countless months looking for a new role. It was hard not to get utterly depressed when you wouldn't even receive an acknowledgement of your application. With all the layoffs and so few roles available, everyone was scrambling to get a job. It was brutal. It wasn't – and still isn't – uncommon to see fellow devs' heartbreaking posts on LinkedIn begging for work, stating that they're 'running out of time'. These were highly qualified workers, often coming from senior roles in both indie and AAA studios, seeking *any* job they could get. And I mean any.

The need to get any work to survive meant that workers couldn't afford to dismiss studios known to get things done through the dreaded 'crunch'. This is something that the industry is notorious for. Crunch is when workers engage in a period of intense, often unpaid overtime, reaching levels of sixty to a hundred hours a week, to meet deadlines. The result is that workers end up being burnt out, often coupled with health issues, and the quality of the actual work will go down.

Unfortunately, this largely exploitative and detrimental practice is often a result of unrealistic deadlines and poor project planning. But when you've no money to pay the bills, no foreseeable offers on the horizon, and with your mental health already shattered with the job hunt, it's easy to see why one may have to forgo their ethical stances with such temptation of any bit of work. There's no luxury in choosing a job you might like these days; it chooses you.

Not only that, but there's the personal toll. I was lucky that I had some savings, and I had the support of my husband, but if there was anything I hated it was being a burden to anyone, and that's what I felt like on the job hunt. Even though my husband was able to support us both, trying to muster the energy to keep facing rejection was taxing. And I was also embarrassed. Here I was, someone who I thought was a highly qualified person, unable to find any role. What did that say about me?

I found myself considering going back to education. Was that even right for me? I didn't know, but I felt at a total loss for what to do next. Most of my former colleagues were in the same boat searching for work, and none of us seemed to be able to find the way forward.

At my wits' end, somehow through the fog of it all, I caught the attention of Gambrinous, an indie Irish studio that reached out to me seeking a producer. Knowing an interview was precious, I did my research and was pleased to see that they were committed to a four-day week, as well as commitments to provide staff with living wages. I felt the strong will to succeed (or at least give a great interview). I was proud to be their Lead Producer, and we shipped our gothic horror game *Eyes of Hellfire* into early access in 2025.

So, do you still want to make games? Yes? OK, then just start! Thankfully, the internet is ripe with ways on how to begin, even if it is no easy feat. But remember, if you've said for years that you've always wanted to work in this industry but never made a game yourself or contributed to one, you more than likely have a passion for playing games rather than making them. And that's OK too; we need players!

Because games are largely interactive by nature and because of their sheer potential when creating them, it's unsurprising that players latch on to those memorable experiences and think they could create something too. But what they need to realize is that it's those same elements that make games such a chore to create. You're not simply done when a game is shipped. You're still very much reliant on the next form of funding, which may or may not be sourced in the background during the current game's cycle.

Game devs may spend years creating environments, characters and mechanics, only to see it all thrown out to take the game in an entirely different direction because the stakeholders and higher-ups simply don't like it. And guess what, even after all of that work, you might get fired anyway or not even be credited for the thing you worked on. C'est la vie.

The inescapable question of working in games is: is it worth it? Given everything my fellow devs and I go through, from a lack of job security to working on projects that are ragdolled aside, it may seem surprising that we bother to keep going. It's all too easy to forget that behind the shiny video games on your favourite gaming platform are people who have sacrificed heavily to turn their creative vision into reality in an industry where failure is rampant. That's nothing to be scoffed at. It's also far too easy for gamers to comment on game developers' posts demanding to know why their creative work, often spanning three to five years, will cost them €40, and why it isn't just free.

Creating a high-quality game in today's fiercely competitive market requires an enormous amount of work, whether it's an indie team working on their first title, a solo dev learning all aspects of game dev or a mammoth effort spanning hundreds of employees. And for most game devs, it's all come at a significant cost. You may forgive us if we do not greet praise immediately with ecstatic enthusiasm. But a little understanding and grace from gamers would go a long way.

To survive burnout, devs must ensure that their personal happiness is as important as their professional output. Wherever you are in the world, and if it's possible, consider joining a game dev union. A good union will fight for things like:

- Fair and just wages, as well as pay transparency
- The end of 'crunch' culture and unpaid overtime
- The end of harassment and intimidation in the industry

There is no need to romanticize long work hours just for the sake of being 'passionate' about working in games. After all, the public doesn't see the shared bond that we game devs have and the extreme crunching that we do; they simply see GAME NAME.

I asked earlier if working in games is worth it. You're probably not surprised that I'm answering with both 'yes' and 'no'. I feel that for it to be 'worth it' depends entirely on your own aspirations, high tolerance for non-stop challenges and the ability to accept that the work-life-balance dream is not achievable without sacrifices. It's the most demanding industry I've worked in, but I have not felt prouder guiding my team's work and seeing our games come to fruition.

The bond we game devs have from AAA to indie games is undeniably strong. Our bond is mingled with all the sweat and tears that got us there, and we deserve better. Seeing the final product of an actual game is strangely unbelievable because it has emerged from the impossible, from chaos. But it has emerged, albeit very, very slowly, despite it all.

CHILDISH THINGS: MY LIFE IN COMPUTER GAMES

Rob Doyle

Jet Set Willy

The first computer we had in my family was a Commodore 64. I only remember using it to play games. You loaded them on cassette in a separate, cream-coloured unit connected by cable to the grey keyboard (a few elite games were loaded by cartridge, plugged in at the back). I sometimes feel that the Commodore 64 represents the apex of my gaming life, a lost kingdom that recedes into the mists so that now, three decades on, I struggle to name more than a handful of titles: *Shinobi, Battleships, Paperboy, Bubble Bobble, Ghouls 'n Ghosts, Spy vs Spy*. I'd be committing a fallacy of nostalgia if I were to suggest that the games back then were *better* than those of subsequent generations, and downright deluded if I said they were more sophisticated. No – the games on the Commodore 64 feel sacred to me because I experienced them with the virginal conscious-ness of a child. At no subsequent stage of life do the games we play – or the songs on the radio, or the cartoons and films we see – evoke emotions that flow so readily back-wards to the womb, and outwards to the infinite.

What I recall best about the early platformer *Jet Set Willy*, beyond the sense of mystery it aroused, is the soundtrack: a looping MIDI rendition of what I now recognize as Beethoven's Bagatelle No. 25 in A minor (commonly, *'Für Elise'*). The wistful delicacy of this composition – the longing that pours through its notes, even in MIDI's harsh metallic tones – remains interwo-ven in my mind with Willy's roam through a seemingly endless 2D mansion populated by glitchy foes. Like all the games my elder brother and I played on the Commodore, *Jet Set Willy* was in colour, which was not the case down the road with my friend James's Amstrad. That had a green screen: the only colours were shades of green. On both the Amstrad and the Commodore, one or two players played using joysticks plugged into ports at the back. As the word suggests, the joysticks were pleas-ingly phallic, tactile objects – tugging and wiggling at them seems, in hindsight, a kind of training.

I recognize my devotion to the Commodore 64 as the root cause of my enduring aversion to sunny days, these sharp pangs of melancholy at the onset of spring. During my childhood, whenever the sun came out my mother would intrude on my game playing to tell me I shouldn't be stuck inside on such a fine day. I'd be banished from my indoor sanctuary, cast out into the pitiless sunlight.

Because there wasn't much to do in the part of Dublin where I'm from other than be harassed by future gangland big-shots, or play nervous games of football in the park, eyeing each pack of approaching figures for potential ball-thieves, I resented these afternoon exiles. A grey sky meant a day of peace and pleasure, of being left alone – and somehow still does.

Mortal Kombat

After the Commodore 64 we upgraded to our first proper games console, the Sega Mega Drive. What were the great Mega Drive games? The obvious classic is Sega's flagship *Sonic the Hedgehog* (and its first sequel), which deserves its iconic status. While not the most compulsive of games, *Ecco the Dolphin* evoked a primordial loneliness, a haunting deep-sea sense of the remote and the nonhuman. Even now, watching long-play videos of Ecco swimming through the fathomless abyss touches something in a distant psychic region, a shiver of Arctic cold at once disquieting and alluring. On the other end of the eco-contemplative spectrum, *Streets of Rage 2* was an engrossingly mindless, scrolling beat-em-up – memorable for how, when the bareknuckle ghetto brawling got too intense, you could call in an airstrike.

Mortal Kombat came out when I was nine. It was a craze, a furore, a classroom buzz. That game delivered my first taste of controversy, transgression. The one-on-one fighter boasted such edgy innovations as splashes of blood and, notoriously, 'Fatalities', by which, after being commanded to *FINISH HIM!*, you executed your opponent with a bespoke 'death-move': Johnny Cage decapitated them with an uppercut; Scorpion peeled back his pre-Covid face-mask and incinerated them with a breath of flame, and so on. Among the dozen or so fight backdrops was 'The Pit'. Here, combatants duked it out under moonlight on a narrow stone ledge, high above a concrete floor bristling with steel spikes. As a finishing move, you had the option of upper-cutting your foe and watching his body plunge over the ledge to be impaled on the spikes below, where it would twitch and spurt globules of bright red blood.

At the time there was much ado about how all this unprecedented video game brutality would warp our minds, turn us into hardened and soulless thugs. In the US, congressional hearings on violence in *Mortal Kombat* and a handful of other games led to the establishment of a content ratings system. In hindsight, it's possible that the controversy – which, like all controversies, carried a giddy erotic charge – was encouraged or even manufac-tured by the game's producers. At the very least, they ben-efited from it, because of course we all had to have *Mortal Kombat*. At school we shared cheats and special move combos with the same fervour that, a year or so later, would see us huddle around in the yard looking at Conor McCabe's samizdat porn magazines.

The obvious reaction now is to smile at such censori-ous naivety — all that panic over a 2D fighting game! But let me voice here the not entirely unserious suggestion that *they really did screw us up* — *Mortal Kombat* and the increasingly brutal games that followed in its wake. At least, they may count as one among a constellation of factors explaining why my psyche is unquestionably darker, more troubled and sad, than that of my father, which was nourished in its formation not by *Crusader: No Remorse* or *Splatterhouse*, but by football on the street, games of chasing, jokes and stories.

Command & Conquer

'Even the word computer sounds backwards and dumb', says corporate theory-shaman Vija Kinski in Don DeLillo's novel *Cosmopolis*, published in 2003 when computers already seemed 'just about dead as distinct units' and were 'melting into the texture of everyday life'. My father bought our first recognizably modern PC in the mid-1990s. From the outset he laid down a rule: the PC would not be used primarily as a games machine. He put a limit on the time my brother and I could spend gaming (a gerund which did not become commonplace until this century: to us it was always *playing computer games*). He hoped we would make use of the educational and self-developmental capacities of the PC, with its early Windows OS and pre-Quantum processor. And we *did* use the PC for more than playing games. In fact, I was more computer-literate then than I am now, adept at behind-the-interface problem-solving and rudimentary coding. In this regard, the PC *was* a game: bugs and crashes were puzzles, while the management of memory and RAM and the organizing of files made its administration into a meta version of the management sims I played on it like *Theme Park* or *Championship Manager*. Then there were the hundreds of hours I spent on MS Paint, applying painstaking detail to forest landscapes and UFO pictures (I was big on *The X Files* during this period), which I'd save on carefully labelled floppy disks.

On a CD-ROM that came free with a computer magazine, we acquired a demo of the real-time strategy game *Command & Conquer*. The demo included only the first two levels, but somehow this didn't matter – playing and replaying the two levels was so exciting that owning the full game seemed an unthinkable luxury.

Command & Conquer was set in a bellicose alternate reality in which a UN-backed military coalition waged war on a millenarian cult. You started each mission with just a few infantrymen, a Humvee or two, and a mobile power station. The first step was to find a suitable location to deploy the station and build your base. Then you could begin harvesting Tiberium, the terraforming mineral that spread in clusters on the grey, stony landscape, which started out dark and was gradually unveiled as you sent out troops on reconnaissance sorties. With minerals gathered and processed in refineries, you could begin erecting barracks and factories and assembling an army.

The territory was secured only when the last enemy soldier was hunted down and exterminated, and all enemy structures were appropriated or destroyed. The frantic action played out to a driving industrial-metal soundtrack (composed by one Frank Klepacki, who would gain lofty status in the industry, scoring sequels and expansion packs that followed the original 1995 game). My father may have been wary of too much game-time undermining our education, but I'm tempted to say that in some sense *Command & Conquer was* an education. At the very least, that game – the two missions I replayed endlessly – absolutely did not make me dumber.

Driver

Everybody knows *Grand Theft Auto*. I even set a whole chapter in one of my novels inside *GTA III*. But who among us still speaks about *Driver*? To me it's the superior game but, like an artist of unappreciated genius forced to watch an imitator bask in glory, it was eclipsed by the *GTA* franchise that began as an overhead, 2D steer-and-shoot, but by its third instalment in 2001 had evolved into the open-world, 3D format *Driver* established in 1999 (with the 'camera' behind and a little above the car). Actually, it seems that *Driver*'s genius is not so unacknowledged after all: the website Ranker grants it top place on a list of the best games on the original PlayStation. The list seems suspect in that I don't recognize most of the titles, but then, writing this essay has been a process of discovering how much I've forgotten or misremembered (I wish I hadn't watched a play-through of *Jet Set Willy* – that's *not* how it's meant to look). The truth is, I scarcely recall owning a PS1, but we must have done, because I *do* remember *Driver*, as elegant and satisfying as any game I've known.

You played as a getaway driver – really an undercover cop, intent on bringing down a crime family. Moral turpitude ensued as you abetted hits and heists in various cities, most memorably San Francisco, whose steep tram-lined streets allowed you to soar through the air and clatter down ahead of oncoming squad cars (the game was openly indebted to classic car-chase movies like *Bullitt* and *The French Connection*). You cruised where you liked by day and night, rendezvousing with gangsters in shipping yards or outwitting cops amid derelict warehouses. We remember games fondly the same way we remember people fondly: in proportion to how good they make us feel about ourselves. Few games match the sense of skill, flair and outright coolness *Driver* bestowed when, with the deftest tap on the brakes, you took a corner at high speed, or pulled a 180 and accelerated between two cop cars hot on your tail, switching to reverse view to watch them swerve, collide and flip.

The games we grow up on colour our imaginations — and if we become writers, our output will be informed by these glamorous cultural products. I wonder if the diminished importance of *entertainment* in contemporary literature is a corollary of the emergence of video games: conscious that more electrifying modes of entertainment are to be found elsewhere, writers can de-emphasize that aspect of their work to focus on doing with prose what only prose can do. Conversely, these days it may be that *games* are focusing less on entertainment, becoming more ambitious, ambiguous, literary. But we're getting ahead of ourselves, because where this narrative left off, I was just about to finish *Driver*, put down the controller, and go to college.

One-Dimensional Man

We did upgrade to a PlayStation 2 in my house, but I don't think of it as having been *my* console so much as my little brother's, who is seven years my younger and thus part of a later generation of gamers. I played the console a fair bit while living at home during college (honourable mention must go to *Minority Report: Everybody Runs*, a film tie-in I regarded as criminally underrated). But I did so with new restlessness: I was starting to feel that it was time, as St Paul exhorted the Corinthians, to 'put away childish things'. I knew that games would become increasingly sophisticated and seductive, and because I had intellectual and creative ambitions, it was imperative that I abandon their womblike shelter and make something of myself in the non-virtual world, such as it is. To fail to do so would be to succumb to what Herbert Marcuse described in *One-Dimensional Man* (which I read around this time) as 'repressive desublimation', and hence be unfit for the diet of difficult books whose mastery was becoming a pillar of my emergent identity.

Thus began the gameless years, a decade and a half in which I occasionally looked in on the evolving universe of games like an urchin with his face pressed against a toy-store window. From a safe distance I admired the advent of the *Assassin's Creed* series and the untrackable proliferation of *Call of Duty* games, while skeptically noting the gradual hegemony of the online multiplayer (I'd always been content with offline games, having little desire to share my immersive worlds with a crowd).

As I made my way in the twenty-first century, I listened with interest to rumours that games were becoming more artful, abstract, feminized, innovative, and I wondered if they were on the cusp of a revolution akin to the modernist overhaul in art and literature a century earlier. But there was too much to do – too many books to read, films to watch, girls to pursue, parties to be had, countries to explore, pages to write.

Bioshock

A couple of winters ago I was living in a stark, bare room in Berlin that a friend described as my 'monk's cell'. Having come to the end of a long creative project, I had sunk into a particularly vicious depression. During this bleak period, I was in frequent online contact with an ex-girlfriend, Roisin, who, when she visited me the following spring, would become my ex-ex-girlfriend. A therapist had once advised me that an underrated source of relief from anxiety and melancholy is distraction. No stranger to spiraling and catastrophic thoughts, Roisin told me that games were her preferred form of distraction-therapy (a few years younger than me, she was not burdened by the early-millennial's uneasiness around playing video games as an adult). She recommended a few indie games accessible via the games platform Steam, and suggested I also try *Bioshock*, a first-person-shooter that was more than a decade old. I soon concluded that *Bioshock* merited its enduring reputation. It looked amazing, for one thing, its twisty plot unfolding in a partially flooded city on the ocean floor, constructed by a crazed billionaire in thrall to the Objectivist philosophy of Ayn Rand. It was funny and charming too – qualities I sensed were scarce amidst the big-budget blaster franchises that dominated the industry skyline. Crucially, *Bioshock*'s eerie, watery atmosphere and tense gunplay really were distracting – I lost myself in it.

And so, I did in my mid-thirties what Paul *didn't* encourage of the Corinthians – I picked back up childish things. Exploring what had been going on in my absence, I found that the rumours were true: indie games were a fertile counterpoint to the big-studio blockbusters, often thrillingly innovative despite graphics engines in the foothills compared to the latter's Himalayan peaks.

There was *The Beginner's Guide* — far from the most exciting of games, but an intriguing, metafictional meditation on creative envy and obsession. *Limbo* was a scrolling 2D indie platformer not all that different from the ones I'd played as a kid on the Commodore 64, though its enchantingly glum aesthetic was in a different cosmos. The same went for *Hotline Miami* and its sequel. These two games (produced by Devolver) fell short of the hyperreal graphics I'd have expected from games produced this far into the century. And yet the top-down, 2D *Hotline* shooters, coloured with *noir* sleaze, superb music and Lynchean surrealism, were demonically playable, extravagantly violent, narratively clever and aesthetically sophisticated in ways that proved things *had* moved on.

Most intriguing to me were the games that, like *Portal*, expanded the limits of what a game or genre could be, warping the laws of time and space while challenging the borders between game and art, narrative and reality. *Portal* and its ilk suggested that, to modify another of Vija Kinski's musings from *Cosmopolis* (she was talking about money), games were going through a phase of abstraction similar to that which painting underwent some decades earlier. Games were talking to themselves.

Superhot

By the time I played the meta-first-person-shooter *Superhot*, I was already familiar with games like *Katana ZERO* and *Braid,* which had features including the ability to manipulate time – reversing or elongating it – and which demonstrated a self-aware attitude to conventions like the player's recurrent death and re-spawning. Such innovations countered the feeling I'd sometimes have that games were not undergoing their modernist moment at all, but were stuck in a loop like players trapped in a level with no end. If you stripped *Call of Duty: Modern Warfare* of its vastly evolved graphics and embellishments, were you not left with the same FPS skeleton on which I'd contentedly been raised, playing *Doom*? And a gorgeous indie hit like *Cuphead*: was it not a more frenetic but otherwise familiar reincarnation of *Sonic the Hedgehog, Aladdin* and the other platformers of my childhood? Perhaps the dazzling effects and relentless action of contemporary games were illusions to keep us blind to the fact that we were trapped, *Matrix*-like, in 1993 – that the future was a thing of the past.

Superhot is a first-person-shooter in the way that Jorge Luis Borges's works are short stories. That is, while Borges's fictions demonstrably belong to a genre, they bear the same relation to that genre as dark matter does to matter. Likewise with *Superhot*: you play it and you immediately know that something new has happened – after years of apparent stagnation, the genre has mutated. There's nothing like it. Or rather, there are hundreds of games that are superficially very much like it – it's a first-person-shooter after all – but *Superhot* stands out by virtue of the foundational question simultaneously posed and answered by its developers: what if there was a shooter that played out *entirely in bullet time*?

The visual effect, whereby the slowing of time allows the player to move with balletic grace, traces a lineage back to the 2001 first-person-shooter *Max Payne*, and before that to its cinematic sources. Most famously, there was *The Matrix*, whose success made of bullet time an action-movie cliché. (Going even further back, Borges's story 'The Secret Miracle' might be considered the ur-text of bullet time.) In games like *Katana ZERO* and *Max Payne*, bullet time was a fleeting special effect that allowed for weaving between bullet-trails, taking out dumbfounded enemies with gunfire or blade. When it wore off, it was back to the fusillade frenzy of real time. In *Superhot*, normal time *is* bullet time. 'Time only moves when you do', runs the game's tagline. But that's not quite accurate. *Superhot*'s genius innovation is that, if you stay still, time moves *very, very* slowly: enemies approach with near-stillness, like murderous statues, so that you can see them coming a mile off even when they're right up in your face. The colour scheme is strikingly spare: enemies are red, guns and weapons are black, and the environment where the shootouts take place is a whitish grey. One hit – by bullet, fist, knife or baseball bat – and you die. Even glancing around while standing still causes time to accelerate, requiring a rigorous economy of motion. Intense shootouts that unfold in a few noisy real-time seconds become intricate choreographies that elapse over minutes and demand great precision. Sound too is elastic: the environment emanates a haunted breathlike ambience, the eeriness enhanced by the featureless faces of your enemies, the nightmare-meaninglessness of their pursuit, and the absence of context to the arenas into which you're hurled with bullet trails already lancing through the air.[1]

---

1 Before I'd even heard of *Superhot*, I found myself inside the game. Last autumn, I went to see my DJ-producer friend Natty play a show at a venue by Görlitzer Park in Kreuzberg. On the way I took a tab of LSD. Afterwards, a group of us moved to an all-night bar on Oranienstraße. Someone offered me a couple of lines of ketamine and I took them. I had never before combined these two substances. As soon as the crushed crystalline shards hit my bloodstream, something unprecedented happened: time slowed to a luminous crawl. A phenomenological shift was effected such as I'd never even come close to experiencing with or without drugs. I remained lucid and self-aware, but my thought processes had far more *time* to contemplate the world around them. I was inhabiting the moment from the inside, as if I'd hacked into the very coding of existence and was at liberty to poke around in the set-design. The cinematic analogy is irresistible: it felt like the scene in *The Matrix* when Morpheus halts time and he and Neo walk down a frozen city street. This was not a transient perceptual transfiguration: it lasted for perhaps an hour of clock time. The walls and surfaces of the bar, the expressions on the faces of the friends I was with: everything appeared more vivid and real than ever, which provoked the astonished sense that it was not real at all — the gnosis of Simulation experienced as first-person ontological shock. I described what was happening to the friend who'd given me the ketamine. She smiled and said, 'Oh, you've unlocked that one. It's amazing, isn't it. How come nobody tells

The ingenious gameplay is matched by a wickedly metafictional narrative. The game begins on an old-school DOS screen, where you exchange messages with a hacker friend. He enthuses about a game in development that he's learned about, *Superhot*, and shares the .exe command to access a rudimentary version. You type the command and enter an unfinished gaming limbo, skeletal and ominous. After you've completed a few slow-motion levels, things begin to get weird. There's a ghost in the machine, a malign System observing your progress and filling your screen with sinister messages. Gradually you're made to feel that you're not playing the game – the game is playing you. You try to quit but the game won't let you (the actual esc key no longer works). Unnerved, you finally get back to the DOS screen and interact once more with your hacker friend. But even your words are not your own, and so you go back into *Superhot*, where now the System no longer warns you off, but lures you deeper in. Eventually, you follow a series of corridors that lead you to a room

---

us about it?' Someone would ask me a question and I felt I had ample time to move around the room, contemplate everyone's body language, admire the elongated synth chords of the song emanating glacially from the sound system, then arrive back to deliver a fully considered response (even if, ketamine being ketamine, actual verbal articulation was markedly trickier to pull off). I watched a trio of hipster-punks dance, laugh and spill their beer at adagio pace. Above them, a white beam of light lanced through layered clouds of cigarette smoke, impacted on the surface of the slowly rotating mirror ball, and exploded in starlike diffusion. It was as if I was witnessing the Platonic form of elegance. When I arrived home that morning, I talked deliriously to my girlfriend about elastic and non-objective time, hardware upgrades, the hidden coding. She feared I'd gone mad. When I was still talking in the same terms the next day, no longer high and demonstrably sane, she became intrigued. On whichever subreddit concerns itself with the metaphysics of ketamine and LSD, she found accounts by others who appeared to have discovered the cheat codes to time and consciousness. 'Reality hacking', they called it.

where, gun in hand, you stalk up behind a figure that you recognize as yourself… sitting at a computer playing *Superhot*.

Abandoned Cities

I played *Superhot* during the winter lockdown in Berlin. It was in most respects a season best forgotten. Confined in our top-floor flat, Roisin and I became twitchy, restive, dejected, our sense of any viable future shrinking. The stimulants and dissociatives for sale on the Telegram app went from being a periodic recreation to a quicksand of addiction and oblivion. For a few jangled weeks, *Superhot* became my sanctuary. Entranced by the game's stark and haunted ambience, I took to recording films on my phone of its slow-motion shoot-outs, with Harold Budd's twenty-minute composition 'Abandoned Cities' (which I was playing continuously in those weeks) droning over the icily affectless gunplay. These iPhone films overlaid with Budd's bleak dronescape began to get under my skin, so that in a sense I could no longer entirely turn off *Superhot* any more than I could cease to hear the glacial foreboding of 'Abandoned Cities' as I lay in bed at night. Red faceless men loomed in the shadows, drifted on the ceiling, flashed across my retinas.

It's something of a commonplace, and entirely accurate, to note that the pandemic accelerated certain societal trends that existed prior to the outbreak, many of them relating to the human-technological interface. Stuck in our homes, we collectively fell even further in thrall to the tech leviathans who dominate the earth, lived out more of our anxious lives through screens. In Western society, there had for years been an incremental collapsing together of the generations, as the traditional markers by which men and women navigated their passage through life – stable careers, nuclear families, home-ownership – disappeared. Now, with no jobs or schools to go to, no pressing responsibilities other than to get through the day, the inhabitants of the West attained the apotheosis of the infantile. There was no sense resisting: if you wanted to play computer games as a man or woman in your thirties, forties, fifties, then you should, because there wasn't much else to do. We were all gamers now, kidults at the end of time. With the shops closed, Roisin and I promised each other the deferred Christmas present of a PlayStation 5, so that together we could give up on the frozen world outside, the failed collective project of adulthood. Ten years older than my father was when he began making a family, I reconciled myself to the pleasures in store as I awaited my return to the dark and enveloping womb that now lay not behind me, but up ahead. Winter's night fell over Europe's silent and abandoned cities, and life became calm and luminous, life became superhot.

WORLD WARRIORS

Stephen Sexton

In the boxing game *Super Punch-Out!!* (Super Nintendo, 1994), sequel to *Mike Tyson's Punch-Out!!* (Nintendo, 1987) and the arcade game *Super Punch-Out!!* (1984), the player wears the gloves of Little Mac. In this plucky underdog's bid to become WVBA (World Video Boxing Association) Champion, he will face sixteen opponents across four circuits: the Minor Circuit, the Major Circuit, the World Circuit and, having claimed these titles, the Special Circuit, with each – as the trajectory of video games usually dictates – increasing in difficulty.

As has ever been the case, with the growing sophistication of processors, memory and computational architectures, so do gameplay, design, and mechanics evolve. So too do characters evolve. In the first of these games, the character is cleft-chinned, dark-haired and nameless, though naturally the player may make their mark on history by entering the three initials by which they will live on in glory in the arcade machine's memory.

By 1987, Little Mac has developed not only a name but a history. He is seventeen years old, from the Bronx, dark-haired and boyish, 107 pounds; tiny on the huge canvas of the ring. He fights in a black leotard with green gloves and shorts. In 1994, owing perhaps to the Super Nintendo's more subtle and expansive colour palette, Little Mac is blue-eyed and blond, with green gloves and blue shorts, bare-chested, as befits a professional boxer.

By 1994, the ring itself is emblazoned with a logo pertaining to the relevant 'circuit'. The audience, cheering at ringside, is made up of a few discernible personalities, repeated in banks of three or four to constitute a roaring spectatorship. In the expensive seats is a man with dark glasses; another with greying hair, another in a red baseball cap; a woman with brown hair. Peppered throughout the crowd, two kinds of cameras are held aloft by spectators, though these will not flash until the final bell has rung.

Unlike many combat games, in which combatants in side profile face each other from the left and right of the screen, the gameplay of *Super Punch-Out!!* offers a perspective that situates the player behind the back of Little Mac, whose definition shifts from a bold opacity to a ghostly translucence when the match begins, allowing the player to see through Little Mac's body to his opponent beyond.

The player learns early on in this game that the optimal strategy is not one of pure offence: this is not a 'brawler'. One is more likely to succeed by looking *through* Little Mac in order to study his opponents' moves: to identify imminent signature attacks, to learn when and what to block and dodge, to know when it's safe to counter-attack. *Super Punch-Out!!* is a perfectly enthralling game: simple and elegant in its gameplay, appropriately challenging, occasionally maddening, but perhaps not groundbreaking.

What makes the game notable, looking back on it, is how it depicts nationality. Even as a child, on his way to pugilistic superstardom, I would wince as the belts accumulated and my opponents ranged from relatively benign stereotypes, such as the milquetoast Gabby Jay (fifty-six, French, with a record of one win and ninety-nine losses) or the burly outdoorsman Bear Hugger (Canadian, very bearded, 440 pounds), to more troubling stereotypes. Piston Hurricane, a twenty-five-year-old Cuban, wears a thin black moustache and warns the player not to get caught in his 'Hurricane Rush' combo. One has the sense that, with this character, his nationality must have been conceived of first, then came the geographical association with Hurricane Alley, and thence a character was born. So far, so (almost) inoffensive.

One's sense of propriety is further challenged upon encountering the Jamaican Bob Charlie, wearing dreadlocks and a bandana, whose manager, calling from ringside, instructs him, 'Bob, time to shuck and jive!' Dragon Chan, a conflation of Jackie Chan and Bruce Lee, is an exponent of kung fu rather than Western boxing, and aims acrobatic high kicks, bouncing off the top ropes for momentum, uttering, all the while, 'kung fu' vocalisations – the 'kiai' familiar to us from martial arts films. We might also look askance at Aran Ryan, the huge-foreheaded Irish boxer, who is possessed of an incredible rage and is inclined to grab his opponent for an up-close punishment.

Mad Clown (the same corpulent sprite as Bear Hugger), Italian, is in conversation with the clowns of Commedia dell'arte. Narcis Prince is a delicate, golden-haired young man from the UK who flies into a rage should you strike his 'beautiful, beautiful face'. Hoy Quarlow is a seventy-eight-year-old Chinese man, curiously lithe for his age, who fights not only with his fists but with a wooden staff.

Among the strangest characters is Heike Kagero, a nineteen-year-old Japanese boxer, who, along with bright pink eyebrows, wears the same shade of pink for eyeshadow, lipstick, gloves and boots. Heike's long grey hair, vigorously whipped, is its own weapon. 'Be gentle with me, please. Hoo, hoo, hoo, hooo!', they say in the pre-match statement. I'm inclined to use the 'they' pronoun to speak of Heike, who is obviously coded as female. In the ring, bare-chested as many other characters, they have, evidently, what we might consider a 'masculine' physique, that is, they are flat-chested and rippling with the pectoral and abdominal muscles we associate with male bodies in peak physical athletic condition. Heike blows kisses.

The game's final two opponents, in the Special Circuit, are brothers Rick and Nick Bruiser. In order to make the two more mysterious and unknowable, neither fighter's age nor nationality is known – question marks replace these particulars. If the opponents one has faced so far range from the comical and novel to the enterprising, rule-bending and troublingly stereotyped, these final opponents are simply evil. Either Bruiser, having blocked a punch and trapped a fist, might slam it with an elbow, disabling 50 per cent of the player's attacking potential. If the player is very unlucky, both fists might become disabled, rendering them useless until the effect wears off.

But for a game that defines its characters, to such an extreme, by nationality, why then are the Bruiser Brothers nation-less? Part of the answer, I suggest, relates to Little Mac and the development of his character, which is enabled by the development of the hardware, from arcade machines to Nintendo to Super Nintendo.

In the first game, without name or nationality, Little Mac is effectively a cipher for the player who has, of course, name and nationality and age and gender and star sign and all the things that make them an individual.

Little Mac subsequently acquires a name and, more importantly, a nationality. Finally, in 1994, he acquires a set of visual attributes we associate with the white, all-American boy ascending into manhood and greatness: he is blond and blue-eyed, clean-cut and athletic. And, given the particular dynamic of this game, the 'behind the back' perspective, the player is inclined to literally see the world through him. He becomes a kind of neutral default, a foil by which the exaggerated and often offensive caricatures of nations can appear more strange and more foreign.

The Bruisers, then, vaguely Slavic, represent something even stranger and more threatening than foreignness: they are stateless. Their evil is one that does not belong to a nation state: they are of the far side of the Berlin Wall, that great, terrifying land of communism. The Cold War was still active, or, to be more precise, still *dormant* at the time of the first two games in this series. By the third, it had, as they say, thawed, though the resonance of such putatively clear-cut concepts of good guys and bad guys, so frequently exploited across action films, lingered in cultural memory.

If the world was about to undergo a series of profound political, economic and cultural recalibrations with the fall of the Berlin Wall in November 1989 and the dissolution of the USSR in 1991, less consequential developments were taking shape in the world of video games. As David Church writes, 'Until the late 1980s, what we would now consider fighting games were often categorized in gaming magazines like *Computer Entertainment* under the broad banner of "sports" games, conflating martial arts, boxing, wrestling, and other full-contact sports as similar athletic endeavors.'

And, he goes on to suggest, games of this period 'increasingly share the beat-em-up's loose narrative context of a good-versus-evil conflict, much as martial-arts films are typically fuelled by far more than the spirit of wholesome competition'.

The *Super Punch-Out!!* series, across its three entries between 1984 and 1994, seems to embody this development: it's nominally a sports game, which is to say what motivates play is the challenge of defeating one's opponents, not so much the experience of a story. However, one can observe the tension between, in Church's distinction, the sports game and the fighting game. To observe the development of Little Mac's character and identity – from nameless boxer, the epitome of the athlete, whose responsibility is to the art of boxing itself, to young New Yorker, fighting sixteen fighters of different nationalities, many of whom are crudely stereotyped – is to observe the development of character, and with character comes politics, history, nationality. One has less of a sense of playing a game and more of a sense of playing a *narrative*.

It's fitting that, in the spirit of those times, the greatest manifestation of evil a young American boxer might face would be a pair of quasi-communist, Slavic-coded, stateless brothers. For all the technological achievement and advancement of processors and circuits, no commensurate sophistication with the soft sciences was to be found among the game designers.

Super Punch-Out!! was not the stand-out sports or fighting game franchise of its generation. That, surely, was the *Street Fighter* franchise, and in particular *Street Fighter II*, released by Capcom in 1991. A handful of variants followed over the next few years, which introduced new characters, increased speed and intensity, updated audio and graphics, and kept the game competitive against newcomers to the fighting genre, especially *Mortal Kombat* (Midway, 1992).

Like the boxing game, *Street Fighter II* suffers from similarly dubious and offensive national stereotypes.

Unlike the boxing game, there is a slight but serviceable narrative. It is this: M. Bison, leader of the criminal Shadaloo organization, seeks to identify new fighters and brainwash them into joining his criminal enterprise to contribute to his plan for world domination. His method is to establish a fighting tournament and have each fighter prove their mettle against one another. Each character has a different motivation to enter the competition and/or to seek to defeat M. Bison. These range from the plausible to the tenuous. Ryu, as near to a protagonist as there is, is close to the true athlete; he enters the contest to improve and refine his Shotokan karate. He is stoic, disciplined. His foil, the American Ken, is Ryu's emotional inverse: arrogant and flashy. Zangief, who fights under the hammer and sickle of the flag of the USSR, wishes only to prove the power of soviet fighters. Dhalsim is an egregious depiction of an Indian holy man who wears a necklace of skulls. His name, Souvik Mukherjee points out, is 'rather unimaginatively named after two food items from Indian cuisine, dal (lentils) and shim (broad beans)'. His wife is named 'Sari'. Of the two characters I find the most compelling, one is Colonel William F. Guile of the US Army, who wishes to avenge the murder of his friend and fellow soldier, Charlie. More on him later. Guile's presentation is that of a soldier but his quest for revenge is purely personal, not professional.

The other compelling character, Blanka, is more mysterious than the others. Blanka is depicted with either blue, green or yellow skin and orange hair. He has fangs, claws, a tattered pair of cargo shorts. He also wears metallic rings around his ankles, suggestive of bondage of some kind. His special moves include wild, rolling cannonball somersaults along both the x and y axis of the screen. He is most notable for his electric shock, channelling 1,000 volts of electricity through his skin. His fighting style is given as 'jungle'. As such, he is not governed by technique and discipline, like Ryu, the practitioner of karate, or E. Honda, the sumo wrestler. Blanka's fighting style is instinctive and vicious. He is an animal.

In the game manual that accompanies the cartridge in its cardboard sleeve – ephemera that is still enchanted and auratic for me – players are given biographical sketches of the characters, alongside their date of birth, height, weight, blood type, nationality and fighting style. Except for all of these facts (no Bruiser brothers question marks here), we learn that 'very little is known about this bizarre fighter from the jungles of Brazil'. Natives have reported, we read on, seeing this 'half-man, half-beast' in the rainforests. Only recently has he come into the cities of Brazil seeking a challenge.

There are contested explanations for Blanka's appearance. Most versions of his origin story claim he was 'once human' and that he survived a plane crash in Brazil as a child. There, overreliance on or exposure to the flora of the jungle caused his skin to turn green. An electrical storm, responsible for downing the plane, is what's given Blanka the ability to generate electric shocks. (Either that or keeping company with electric eels.) Blanka's goal in the tournament is to gain greater exposure – to be seen – in the hope that, should someone recognise him, he might learn something about his past. To put it another way, he might regain a sense of *narrative*.

Indeed, he does: after defeating the final boss, M. Bison, a short cutscene sees a woman rush to his side. She calls him 'Jimmy' and recognises the creature before her as the son she lost as a child, when his plane, 'flying over Brazil', crashed. Moreover, what was until this point ostensibly a metallic shackle around his calf is now revealed to be an 'anklet' his mother had given to him as a birthday present. It has, remarkably, grown to accommodate the bulk of the creature wearing it. Ambiguities abound: 'flying over Brazil', as his mother puts it, suggests that that country was neither origin nor destination. 'Jimmy', to my ear, is not suggestive of a Brazilian name. Blanka, of course, is a variation of 'blanca'; 'white' in Spanish (but not Portuguese).

Ambiguities should abound, for Blanka, stripped of humanity, is monstrous; what's monstrous is what's aberrant. Most immediately, he is aberrant to the eye: his skin has mutated, he has lost many of the behaviours of the human, he fights like a wild beast. But he is also aberrant in the sense that he is without origin or heritage: he has no gym nor dojo, no tradition of sumo, karate, boxing, Muay Thai. We cannot be certain of his nationality, even if his flag is that of Brazil. He is the fact of himself. His reward, such as it is, for winning the tournament, is the restoration of narrative: he is redeemed by his mother's presence, given the dignity of humanity.

Nicholas Ware suggests that Blanka is representative of Japanese racism towards 'ethnically Japanese Brazilian immigrants coming to Japan during the economic boom years to work factory jobs', whose 'Japanese ethnicity gave them easy access to work visas' but whose 'Brazilian culture and Portuguese language use … threatened the perceived homogeneity of Japanese cultural identity'. Patrick Miller, not beating around the bush, said in a round-table discussion: 'because these games were predominantly made by Japanese studios, they could get away with a shit ton of super racist character designs that do not register in a way that Americans are used to'.

Both *Super Punch-Out!!* and *Street Fighter II* are Japanese games (Nintendo and Capcom), and both are concerned with international competition. In their ways, each game reflects a different kind of friendly international competition between the USA and Japan in their respective spheres of West and East. Given the spectacle, the razzle-dazzle of boxing in the United States in the second half of the twentieth century, it is sensible that Little Mac should be an American. Besides, Japan's national sport is sumo wrestling, and while its martial arts are many, boxing is not necessarily one of them. The boxing game has an American hero; *Street Fighter II*'s most likely hero, Ryu, is Japanese.

Each game's representation of nationality also suggests how each nation conceives of itself, what it celebrates and what it considers threatening in both foreign and domestic policy. In *Super Punch-Out!!*, the most offensive 'big bad' is to be found in the Bruiser brothers: stateless, brutish, inscrutable; the Eastern Bloc given boxing gloves. In *Street Fighter II*, its main antagonist,

M. Bison, criminal and possibly criminally insane, is afforded considerably more dignity and humanity than Blanka, whose monstrosity, according to Ware, reflects Japanese insecurities about migration and ethnicity.

Remarkably, the live-action adaptation of *Street Fighter II*, Steven E. de Souza's 1994 film, *Street Fighter*, manages to blend statelessness and monstrosity into one being: Blanka. M. Bison, here General M. Bison, up to his old tricks, has kidnapped 'Allied Nations' aid workers (a thinly disguised United Nations), and has demanded a $20 billion ransom. Magisterial in his final role, Raul Julia plays M. Bison as a Shakespearean-inflected megalomaniac in red leather with a cloak (and cloak chains across his collarbones) and a peaked cap bearing his Nazi-esque winged skull emblem. His crime syndicate is here a militia of heavily armed 'Bison Troopers', with whose force he seeks world domination, which includes an overhaul of the world economy wherein 'each bison dollar will be worth five British pounds', the exchange rate the Bank of England will agree, Bison explains, once he's kidnapped their queen.

Key to this plan for world domination is Bison's ambition to create 'the perfect genetic soldier', a trope common among action movies and video games in the 1990s (*Universal Soldier, Metal Gear Solid*) and in the decades before and after. Prowling through a diorama of 'Bisonopolis' (his world capital, we suspect), he says – in perfect exposition – that these perfect genetic soldiers 'shall march out of my laboratory and sweep away every adversary, every creed, every nation, until the very planet is in the loving grip of the *Pax Bisonica*. His ambition, then, is to eradicate difference and bring to a final end the nation state, a plan that bears some resemblance to the long-held fears of those exercised by the apparently imminent New World Order, itself a particularly American phobia, cognate as it is with a Communist, one-world government.

Opposing M. Bison is American Colonel William F. Guile of the Allied Nations, played by the famously Belgian Jean-Claude Van Damme. While this is not a conflict of nations, the USA leads the alliance in its efforts to restore order to 'Shadaloo', the fictional South East Asian country in which the action unfolds. The echoes of the 1960s and 1970s in Vietnam are palpable and are made explicit by a radio announcer's singsong 'Good Morning Shadaloo'.

If Guile's primary objective is infiltrating the secret base and defanging, arresting and bringing M. Bison to justice, as the world's policeman should, his secondary objective is rescuing his friend Charlie, one of the relief workers kidnapped at the film's outset. In a moment of indiscretion necessary for the plot, Guile gives away this personal relationship just as Bison is inspecting his prisoners. 'Carlos Blanka', he reads from the soldier's dog tag. 'Charlie'. Charlie is immediately taken to the laboratory to commence his genetic transformation into 'super soldier', under the observation of Dr Dhalsim.

Like many movies that made an impression on me when I was young, I'm extremely fond of *Street Fighter*. It is a wonderful mess. With the exception of Raul Julia, much of the acting is cringe-inducing. The translation of video game characters into their live-action counterparts is largely forgivable, even if Guile's role as protagonist and exponent of American military power is jarring. What I find less forgivable is the conflation of two characters: Charlie and Blanka, in a way that effaces both characters' narrative integrity and blends them into a singular, crude political object.

The process of transforming Charlie into Blanka, much like the 'Ludovico Technique' from *A Clockwork Orange*, involves forcing him to watch incessant violent imagery through a visor within an incubation chamber, which itself suggests rebirth. 'When his brain has become a killing machine,' Bison tells Dhalsim, 'my loyal scientists will start on his body.' Ideology first, physicality second. Charlie as Blanka is an amalgamation of the two threats I described earlier, where first world (and American) identity is corrupted into statelessness (Bison's new world order) and humanity is mutated into monstrosity (genetic and ethnic aberration).

Upon encountering his friend, now half-beast, Guile's first instinct, to *help* him, is to execute him, until Dhalsim, full of shame and regret, stops him. 'The real monster's upstairs,' he says. The battle ensues, Bison is defeated, the good guys win, proper order is restored. With Bison's base's self-destruct system counting down, Blanka, too monstrous for the world, and Dhalsim, eager to atone, elect to perish in the underground laboratory of history. They are, after all, in the struggle between axes of power, expendable; their stories, however codified, are irrelevant. They serve – whatever it calls for – the dominant power.

'Only that which narrates can make us understand,' said Susan Sontag in *On Photography*, describing the photograph's incapacity for narrative. Without narrative, we have no sense of time, context or causality. Many of these characters, particularly those like Blanka, who have absent or inconsistent narratives, are thus perpetually Other, subject to all kinds of prejudice and estrangement, beyond understanding, beyond empathy.

Video games are, after all, video games. We can't expect them to enact greater compassion and discernment than the world and the people who produced them. However refined our technologies for visual representation become – games engines, processors, artificial intelligence – no amount of graphical fidelity or high definition will prove revolutionary without corresponding narrative dexterity. There is more than one way to look at the world, and more than two. There are many more versions of history, regardless of what the victors would have you think.

ENDNOTES

Church, D, *Mortal Kombat: Games of Death*. University of Michigan Press 2022. *JSTOR*, https://doi.org/10.3998/mpub.11477677. Accessed 25 Aug. 2025.

Patterson, C, (editor), Fickle, T (editor), *Made in Asia/America: Why Video Games Were Never (Really) about Us*. Duke University Press 2024.

Ware, N, 'A Whirl of Warriors: Character and Competition in Street Fighter.' In *The Play versus Story Divide in Game Studies*, edited by Matthew Wilhelm Kapell, 158–70. Jefferson, NC: McFarland 2016.

CONTRIBUTORS

Sheila Armstrong is a writer from the north-west of Ireland. She is the author of *How To Gut A Fish*, a collection of short stories, and two novels, *Falling Animals* and *The Red Mouth*.

Rob Doyle is the Dublin-born author of several internationally acclaimed books: *Threshold*, *Autobibliography*, *This Is the Ritual*, *Here Are the Young Men*, which has been adapted for film starring Anya Taylor-Joy, and most recently, *Cameo* (W&N). His writing has appeared in the *New York Times*, *Observer*, *New Statesman*, *Dublin Review* and many other publications. His books have been nominated for various prizes and translated into several languages.

Joe Dunthorne is a poet and novelist. His debut novel, *Submarine*, was translated into fifteen languages and made into an award-winning film. His second novel, *Wild Abandon*, won the Royal Society of Literature's Encore Award. His debut poetry collection, *O Positive*, was published by Faber & Faber in 2019. His latest book, *Children of Radium* – a memoir about family and chemical weapons – was published in April 2025 and adapted into an award-winning BBC podcast. He was born in Swansea and lives in London.

Dr. Donal Fullam is a researcher and artist who focuses on art in contemporary algorithmic culture, automation, and human-computer creative relationships. With NAMACO, he makes video games that explore urgent social issues and create interactive spaces to confront the logic of neoliberal capitalism. He has been involved in underground DIY punk for over 20 years, playing and recording with many different bands throughout Ireland and around the world in a variety of legal and extra-legal settings. His work can be found at www.namaco-industries.net

Úna-Minh Kavanagh is a queer, Irish-Asian person of colour from Ireland. She is a Solo Game Developer, Game Producer, Writer, and Author who creates small, strange and story-rich games. Úna-Minh loves writing interactive fiction, uplifting people, D&D, and, of course, playing games. She's shipped two indie titles, *Saltsea Chronicles* (Die Gute Fabrik - 2023), *Eyes of Hellfire* (Gambrinous - 2025), and project manages a team that has officially localised indie titles such as *Among Us* and *VVVVVV*, into the Irish language. Find out more about her: https://unaminhkavanagh.com/

Roisin Kiberd is the author of *The Most Normal Woman: Essays on Appearances* (coming in August 2026), and *The Disconnect: A Personal Journey Through the Internet* (2021). She has written for the *New York Times*, *The Dublin Review*, *The Stinging Fly*, *Winter Papers* and others, and teaches creative writing at the University of Galway.

Anna Loughran lives in England and is working toward a PhD in Creative Writing at Loughborough University.

Darragh McCausland is a writer from Kells, County Meath. He has had fiction and non fiction published in various journals and anthologies from Ireland and further afield. He grew up on RPGs.

John Patrick McHugh is from Galway. His work has appeared in the *Stinging Fly*, *Winter Papers*, *Banshee*, *Tolka*, and *Granta* and been broadcast on BBC Radio 3. He is the author of the short story collection *Pure Gold* and the novel *Fun and Games*.

Lisa McInerney is the author of three novels: *The Glorious Heresies, The Blood Miracles* and *The Rules of Revelation*. She has won the Women's Prize for Fiction, the Desmond Elliott Prize, the RSL Encore Award and the Premio Edoardo Kihlgren for European literature. She is published in 13 languages. She is the editor of *The Stinging Fly*, and teaches Creative Writing at the University of Galway.

Chandrika Narayanan-Mohan is an Irish-Indian writer, performer, and cultural consultant, published by *Banshee, The Stinging Fly*, Poetry Ireland, and others. She has been artist-in-residence for several science initiatives and is a Skein Press 'Play it Forward' Fellow. Her debut poetry collection is being published with Dedalus Press in 2026.

Brenda Romero is a writer and game designer from Galway via New York whose work spans fiction, essays, and the evolving field of playable literature. A graduate of the

Creative Writing programme at University of Galway, her writing has appeared in *The Stinging Fly*, *Tolka*, and *The Dublin Review*. She is the author of multiple books and is currently a PhD student in English at Trinity College Dublin, where her research explores the intersections of narrative, interactivity, and storytelling in contemporary media.

Stephen Sexton's first book, *If All the World and Love Were Young* was the winner of the Forward Prize for Best First Collection in 2019. He was awarded the E.M. Forster Award from the American Academy of Arts and Letters and the Rooney Prize for Irish Literature in 2020. *Cheryl's Destinies* was published in 2021, and was shortlisted for the Forward Prize for Best Collection.

Paul Whyte is a Tipperary born writer currently living in Dublin with his wife and 3 children. His debut novel *Harrow the Boys* (2020) was published by Maverick House in Ireland and the UK. His short fiction, essays and articles have been published in places like *The Moth*, *The Pig's Back*, *The Irish Examiner*, *The Lonely Crowd* and more.

Dean Fee is a writer and editor based in Donegal. His work has been published in *The Dublin Review*, *The Stinging Fly*, *Banshee*, on BBC Radio and many more places. He is a founder and the managing editor of *The Pig's Back* literary journal.

ACKNOWLEDGMENTS

Some of the essays in this anthology were previously published in literary journals and magazines. I would like to thank the editors of those publications for not only allowing me republish the work, but for having the foresight to publish it in the first place. It was from reading these pieces live – so to speak – that gave me the idea for *CTRL*. So, many thanks to *The Stinging Fly, Tolka, The London Review of Books and The Dublin Review*.

Thanks to everyone who helped me along the way or gave me advice, namely Tom Morris, Nidhi Zak/Aria Eipe, and Emily O'Brien. Thanks in particular to my girlfriend Emily who absolutely hates video games but held her silence during my many, many 'research' days. Thanks also to everyone at The Lilliput Press for helping put this book together. It was an easy joy throughout. And thanks finally to anyone I've ever played video games with, be that my friends and family, or just some random person who helped me kill a boar, or allowed me to defeat them in a battle that momentarily gave me a great sense of achievement.

9 781843 519768